CW00750892

DRAGON AGE

THE SILENT GROVE

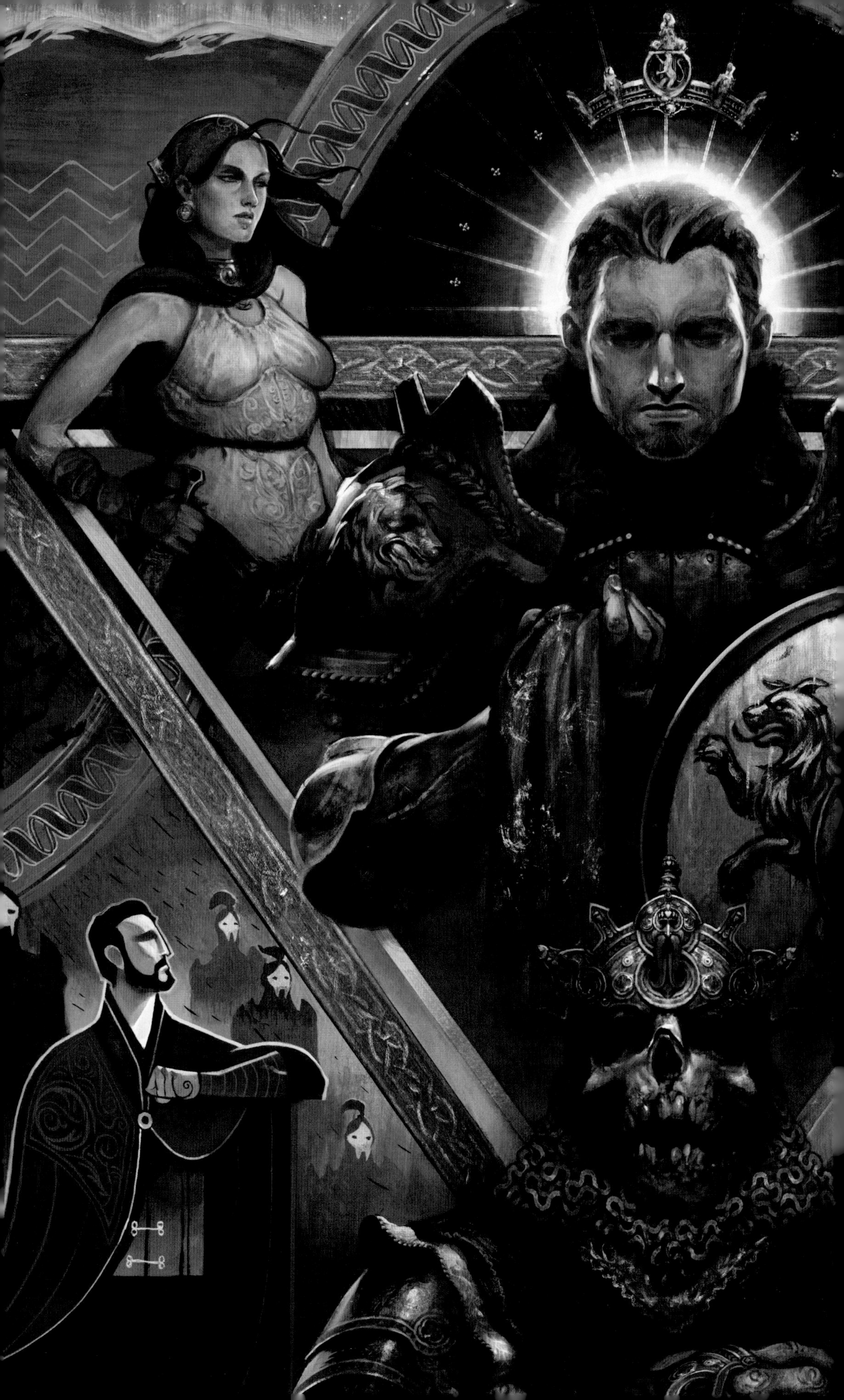

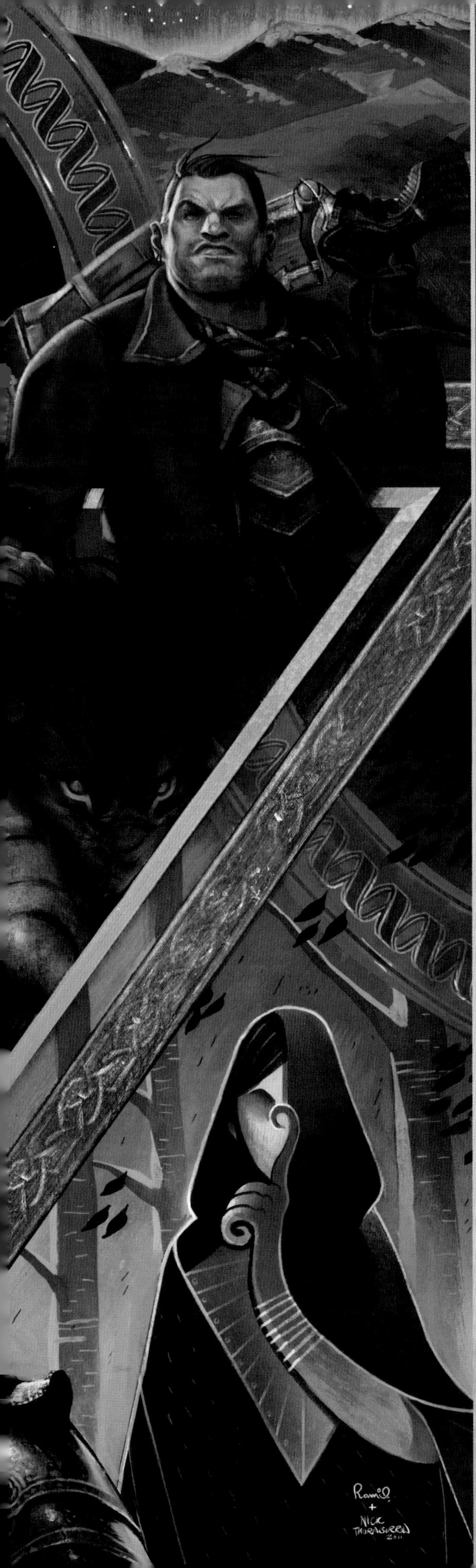

DRAGON AGE™

THE SILENT GROVE

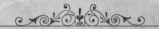

STORY
DAVID GAIDER

SCRIPT
ALEXANDER FREED

ART
CHAD HARDIN

COLORS
MICHAEL ATIYEH

LETTERING
MICHAEL HEISLER

FRONT COVER ART
ANTHONY PALUMBO

TITLE PAGE ILLUSTRATION
RAMIL SUNGA AND
NICK THORNBORROW

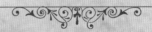

DARK HORSE BOOKS
EA
BIOWARE

PUBLISHER
MIKE RICHARDSON

COLLECTION DESIGNER
ADAM GRANO

ASSISTANT EDITOR
BRENDAN WRIGHT

EDITOR
DAVE MARSHALL

SPECIAL THANKS TO BIOWARE, INCLUDING:
Matthew Goldman, Art Director • Mike Laidlaw, Lead Designer
Aaryn Flynn, Studio GM, BioWare Edmonton • Ray Muzyka and Greg Zeschuk, BioWare Co-Founders

---

DRAGON AGE VOLUME 1: THE SILENT GROVE

This volume collects issues one through six of the Dark Horse digital comic-book miniseries *Dragon Age: The Silent Grove.*

Published by
Dark Horse Books
A division of
Dark Horse Comics, Inc.
10956 SE Main Street
Milwaukie, OR 97222

DarkHorse.com
DragonAge.com

Library of Congress Cataloging-in-Publication Data

Gaider, David.
Dragon age : the silent grove / story, David Gaider ; script, Alexander Freed ; art, Chad Hardin ; colors, Michael Atiyeh ; lettering, Michael Heisler ; cover art, Anthony Palumbo. — 1st ed.
p. cm.
ISBN 978-1-59582-916-0
1. Graphic novels. I. Freed, Alexander. II. Hardin, Chad.
III. Atiyeh, Michael. IV. Heisler, Michael. V. Palumbo, Anthony. VI. Title.
PN6727.G35D73 2012
741.5'973--dc23
2012004654

First edition: July 2012

3 5 7 9 10 8 6 4 2
Printed in China

Almost a decade ago, the terror of the Fifth Blight swept the nation of Ferelden. Civil war soon followed, as King Cailan died in battle against the monstrous darkspawn, and a usurper took his place.

Only the actions of a few heroes—King Cailan's brother Alistair among them—prevented utter devastation. Since then, the new King Alistair has ruled with a steady hand and seen to his homeland's reconstruction.

But Ferelden is not the world, and its troubles thread through distant lands. Today, a ship arrives in a northern port, and its passengers would unearth a secret that could change everything . . .

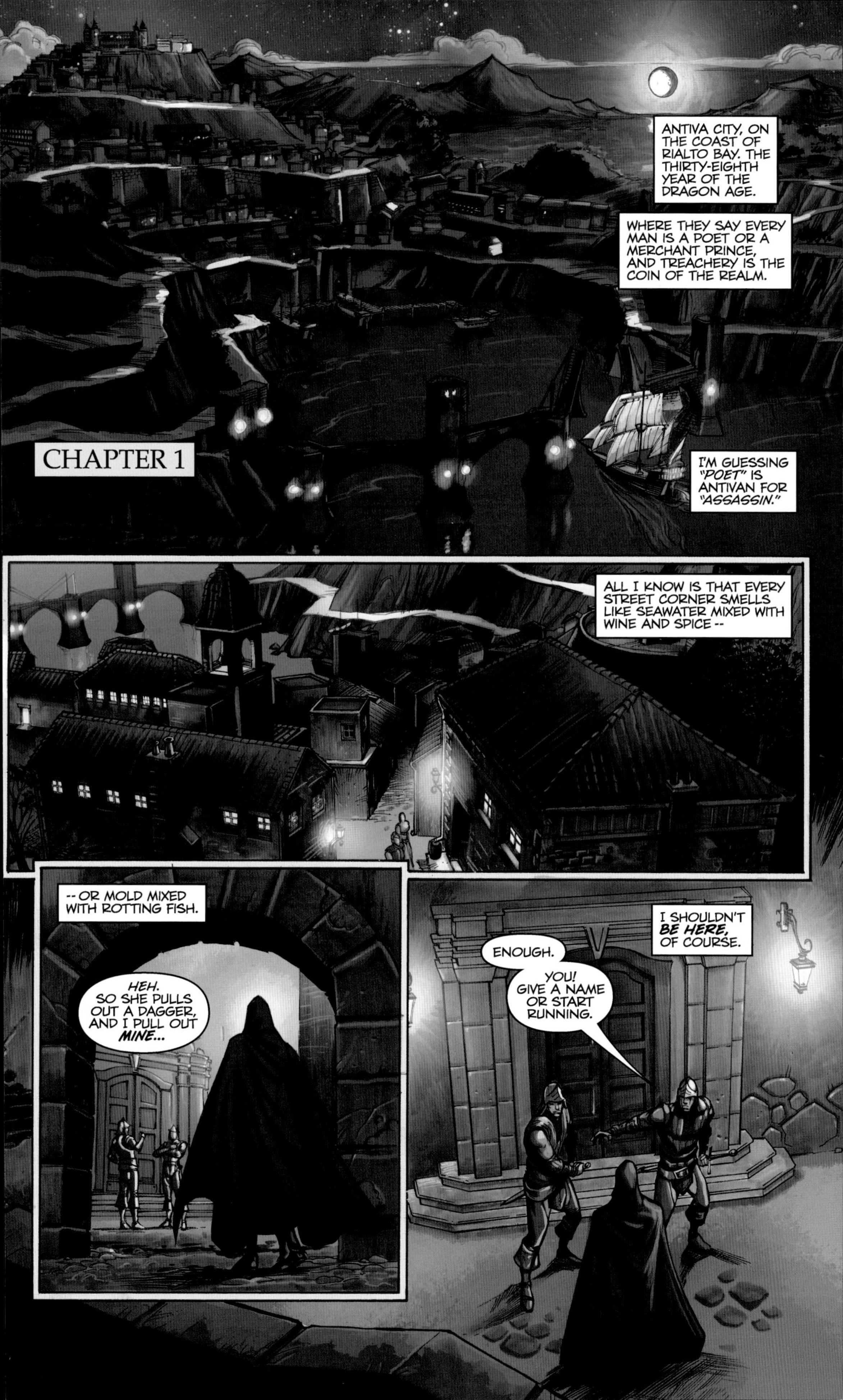
ANTIVA CITY, ON THE COAST OF RIALTO BAY. THE THIRTY-EIGHTH YEAR OF THE DRAGON AGE.
WHERE THEY SAY EVERY MAN IS A POET OR A MERCHANT PRINCE, AND TREACHERY IS THE COIN OF THE REALM.
CHAPTER 1
I'M GUESSING "POET" IS ANTIVAN FOR "ASSASSIN."
ALL I KNOW IS THAT EVERY STREET CORNER SMELLS LIKE SEAWATER MIXED WITH WINE AND SPICE --
-- OR MOLD MIXED WITH ROTTING FISH.
HEH. SO SHE PULLS OUT A DAGGER, AND I PULL OUT MINE...
I SHOULDN'T BE HERE, OF COURSE.
ENOUGH.
YOU! GIVE A NAME OR START RUNNING.

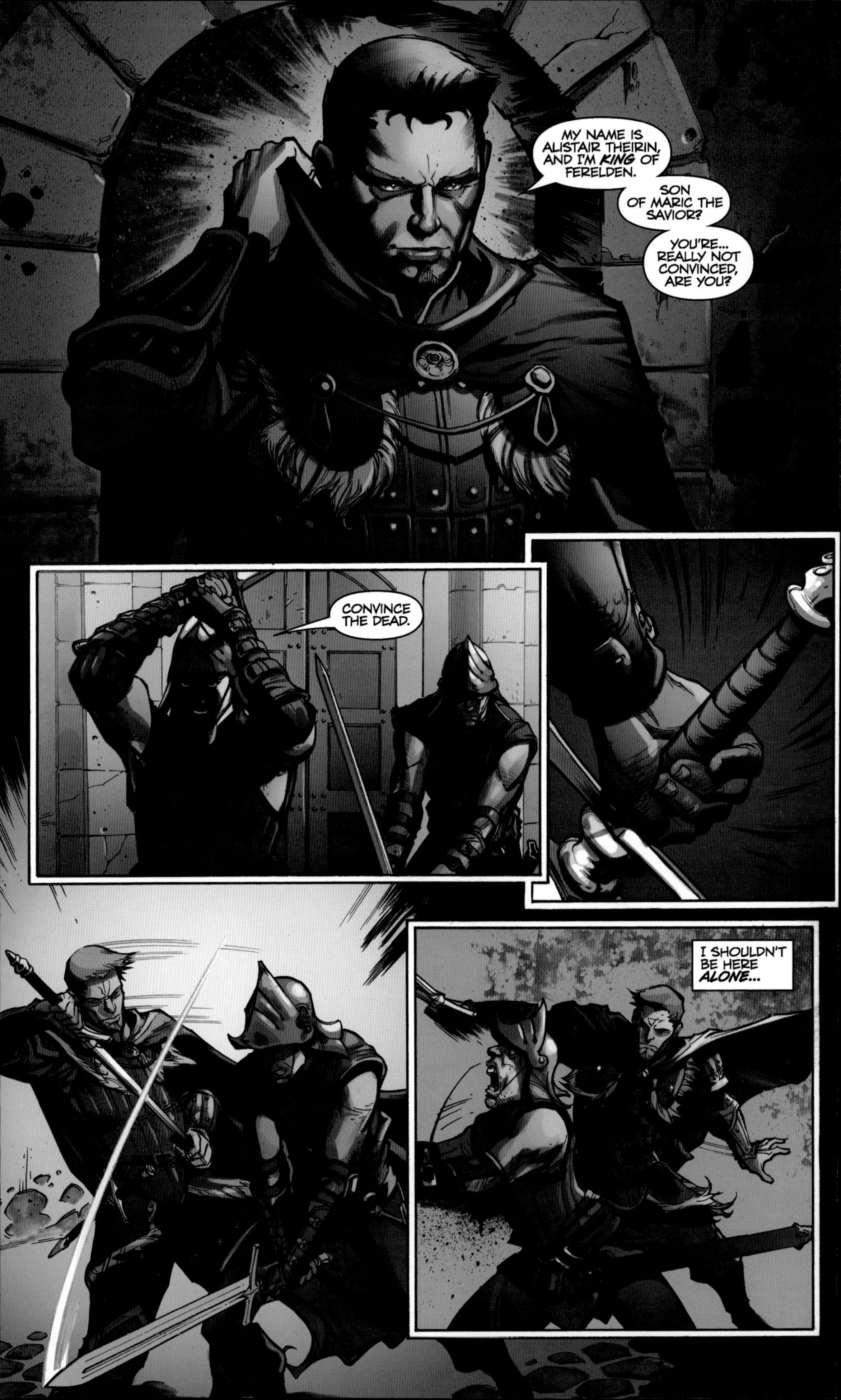
MY NAME IS ALISTAIR THEIRIN, AND I'M KING OF FERELDEN.
SON OF MARIC THE SAVIOR?
YOU'RE... REALLY NOT CONVINCED, ARE YOU?
CONVINCE THE DEAD.
I SHOULDN'T BE HERE ALONE...

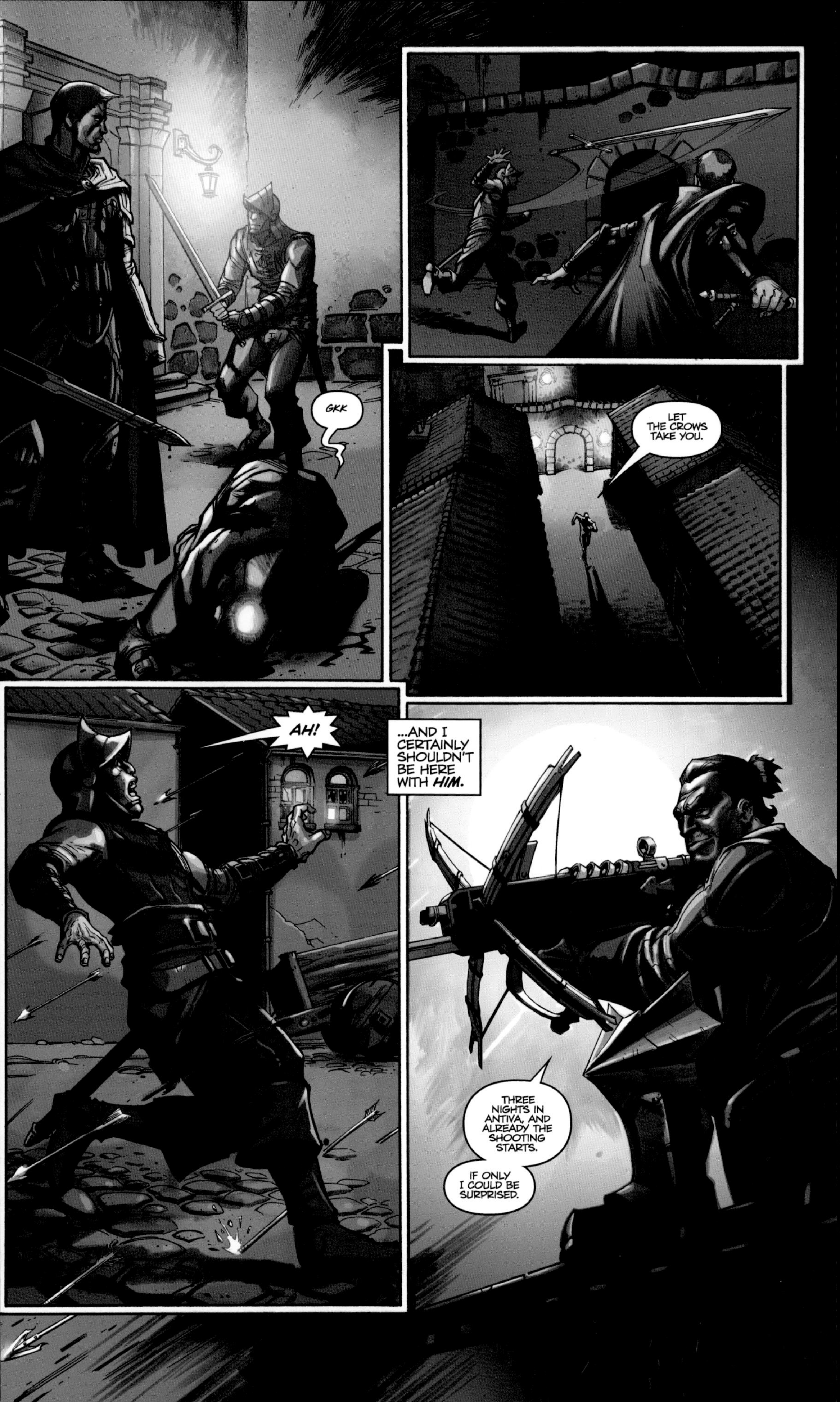
GKK
LET THE CROWS TAKE YOU.
AH!
...AND I CERTAINLY SHOULDN'T BE HERE WITH *HIM*.
THREE NIGHTS IN ANTIVA, AND ALREADY THE SHOOTING STARTS.
IF ONLY I COULD BE SURPRISED.

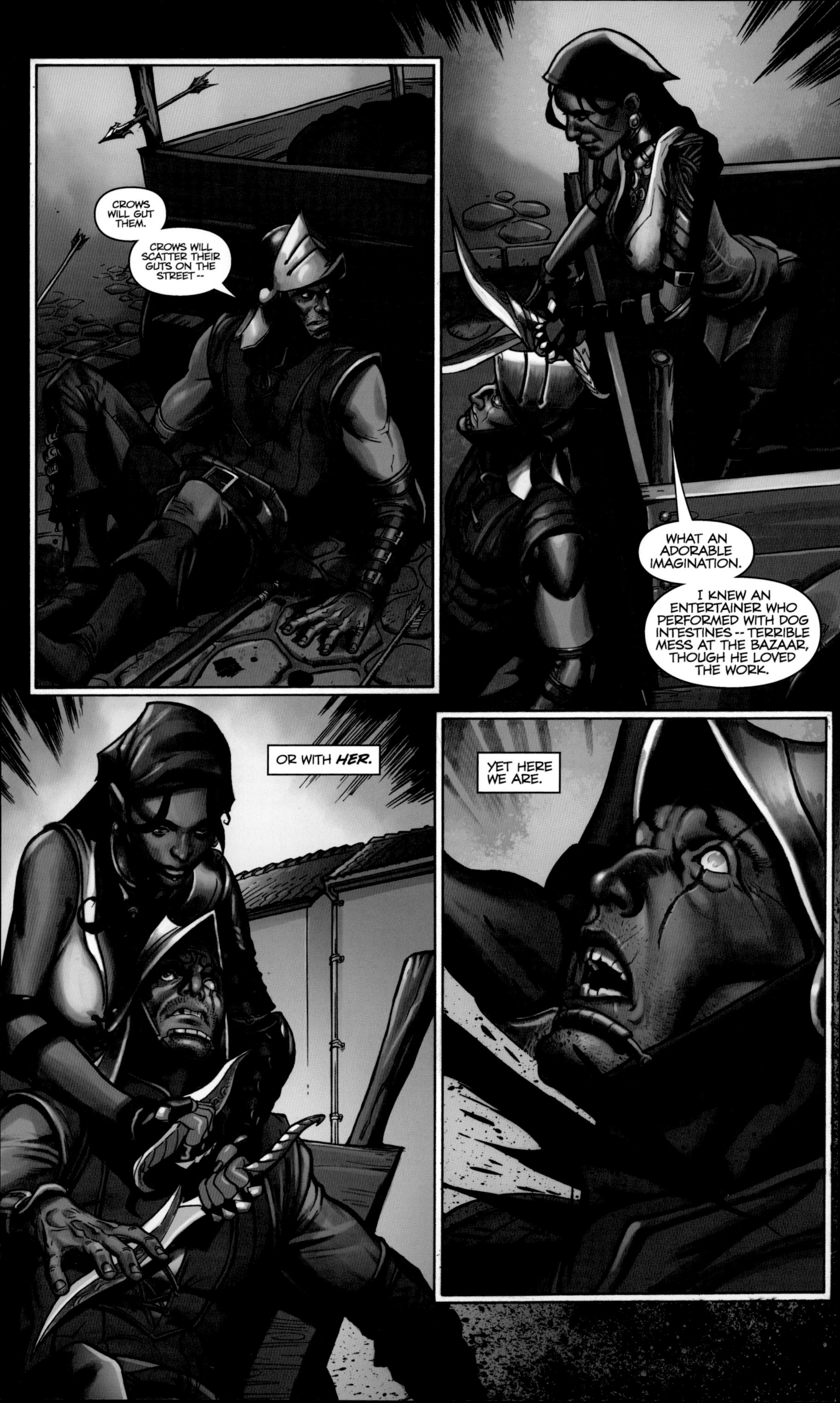

CROWS WILL GUT THEM.
CROWS WILL SCATTER THEIR GUTS ON THE STREET --
WHAT AN ADORABLE IMAGINATION.
I KNEW AN ENTERTAINER WHO PERFORMED WITH DOG INTESTINES -- TERRIBLE MESS AT THE BAZAAR, THOUGH HE LOVED THE WORK.
OR WITH HER.
YET HERE WE ARE.

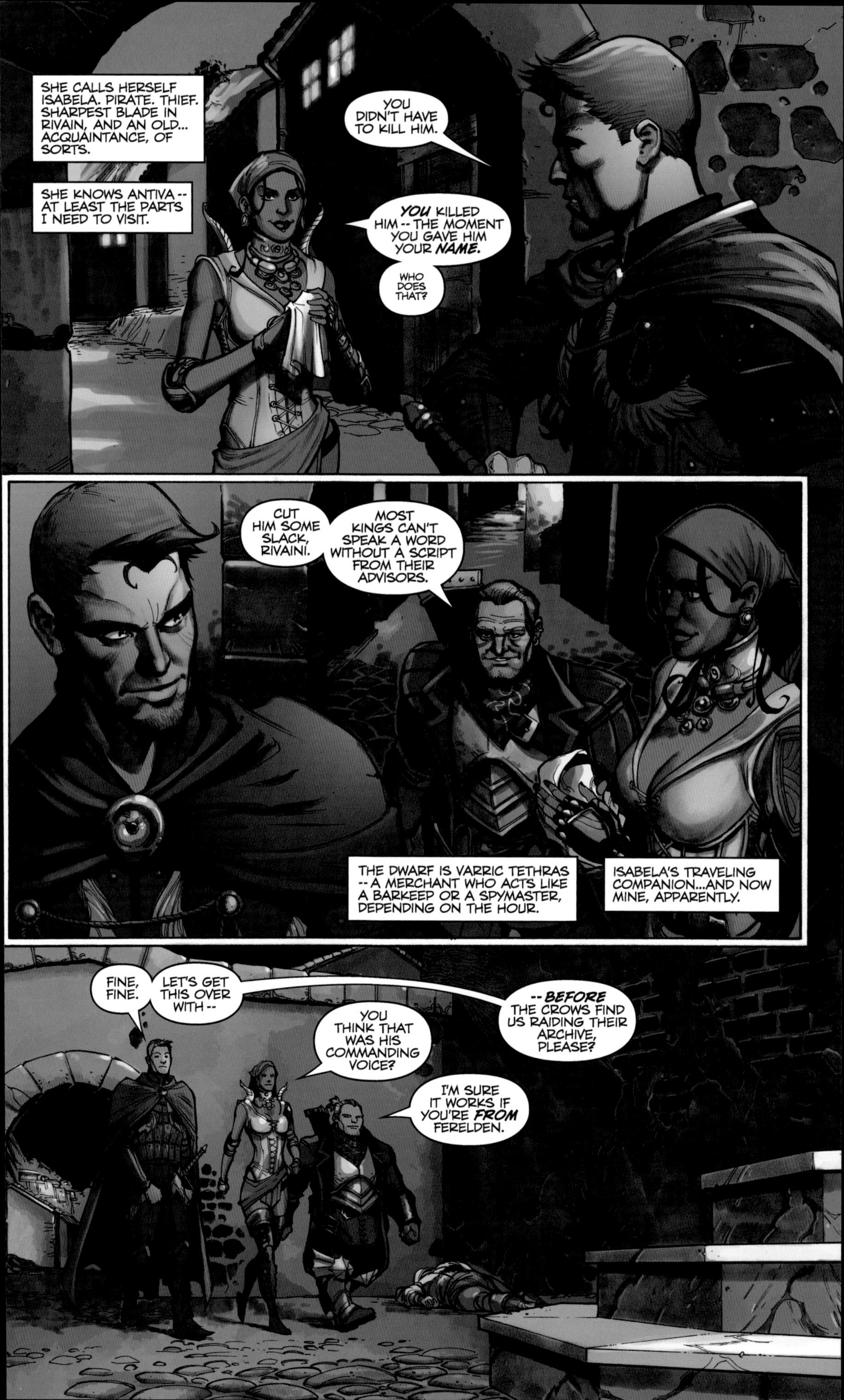
SHE CALLS HERSELF ISABELA. PIRATE. THIEF. SHARPEST BLADE IN RIVAIN, AND AN OLD... ACQUAINTANCE, OF SORTS.
SHE KNOWS ANTIVA -- AT LEAST THE PARTS I NEED TO VISIT.
YOU DIDN'T HAVE TO KILL HIM.
YOU KILLED HIM -- THE MOMENT YOU GAVE HIM YOUR NAME.
WHO DOES THAT?
CUT HIM SOME SLACK, RIVAINI.
MOST KINGS CAN'T SPEAK A WORD WITHOUT A SCRIPT FROM THEIR ADVISORS.
THE DWARF IS VARRIC TETHRAS -- A MERCHANT WHO ACTS LIKE A BARKEEP OR A SPYMASTER, DEPENDING ON THE HOUR.
ISABELA'S TRAVELING COMPANION...AND NOW MINE, APPARENTLY.
FINE, FINE.
LET'S GET THIS OVER WITH --
-- BEFORE THE CROWS FIND US RAIDING THEIR ARCHIVE, PLEASE?
YOU THINK THAT WAS HIS COMMANDING VOICE?
I'M SURE IT WORKS IF YOU'RE FROM FERELDEN.

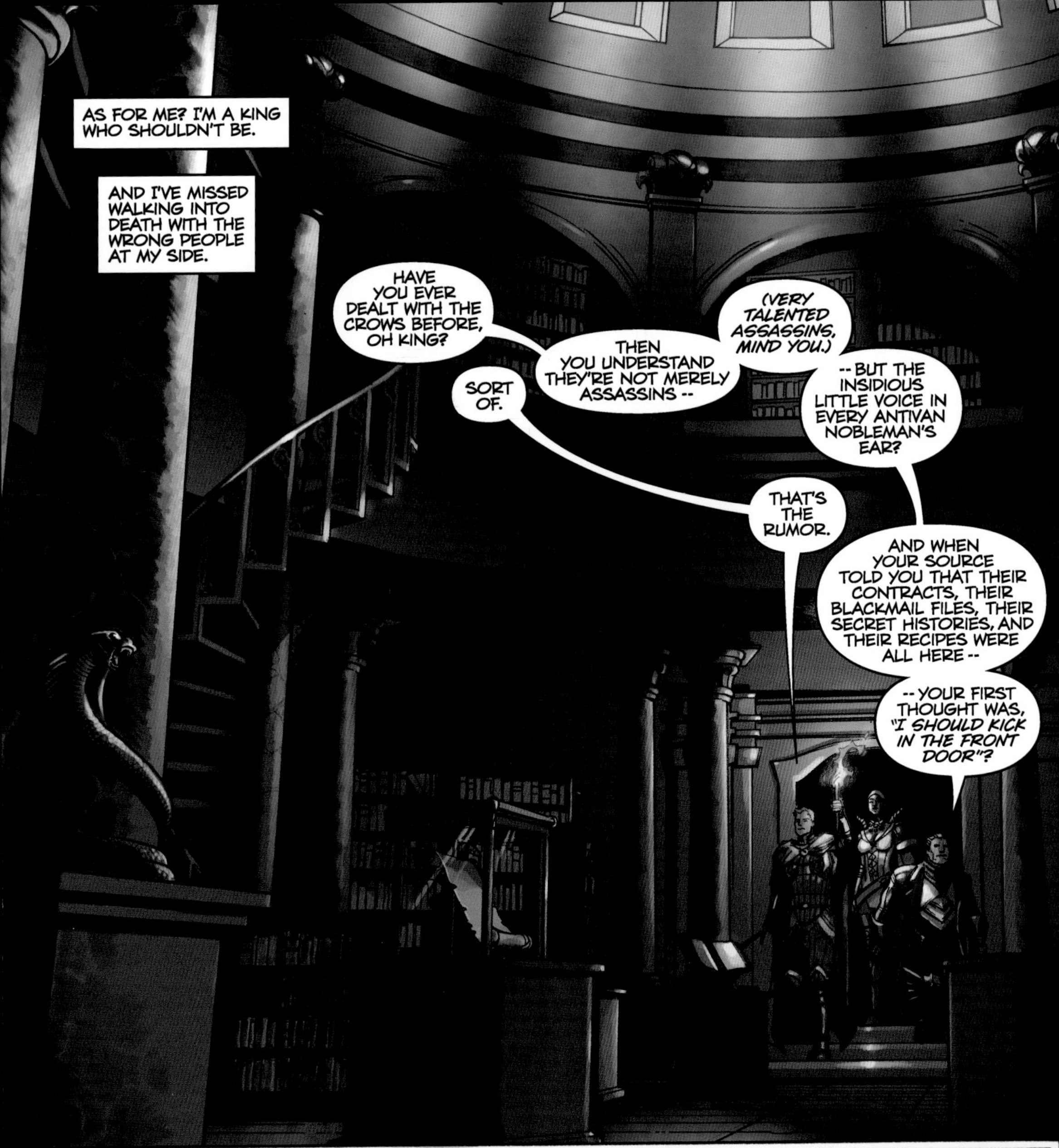
AS FOR ME? I'M A KING WHO SHOULDN'T BE.
AND I'VE MISSED WALKING INTO DEATH WITH THE WRONG PEOPLE AT MY SIDE.
HAVE YOU EVER DEALT WITH THE CROWS BEFORE, OH KING?
SORT OF.
THEN YOU UNDERSTAND THEY'RE NOT MERELY ASSASSINS --
(VERY TALENTED ASSASSINS, MIND YOU.)
-- BUT THE INSIDIOUS LITTLE VOICE IN EVERY ANTIVAN NOBLEMAN'S EAR?
THAT'S THE RUMOR.
AND WHEN YOUR SOURCE TOLD YOU THAT THEIR CONTRACTS, THEIR BLACKMAIL FILES, THEIR SECRET HISTORIES, AND THEIR RECIPES WERE ALL HERE --
-- YOUR FIRST THOUGHT WAS, *"I SHOULD KICK IN THE FRONT DOOR"*?

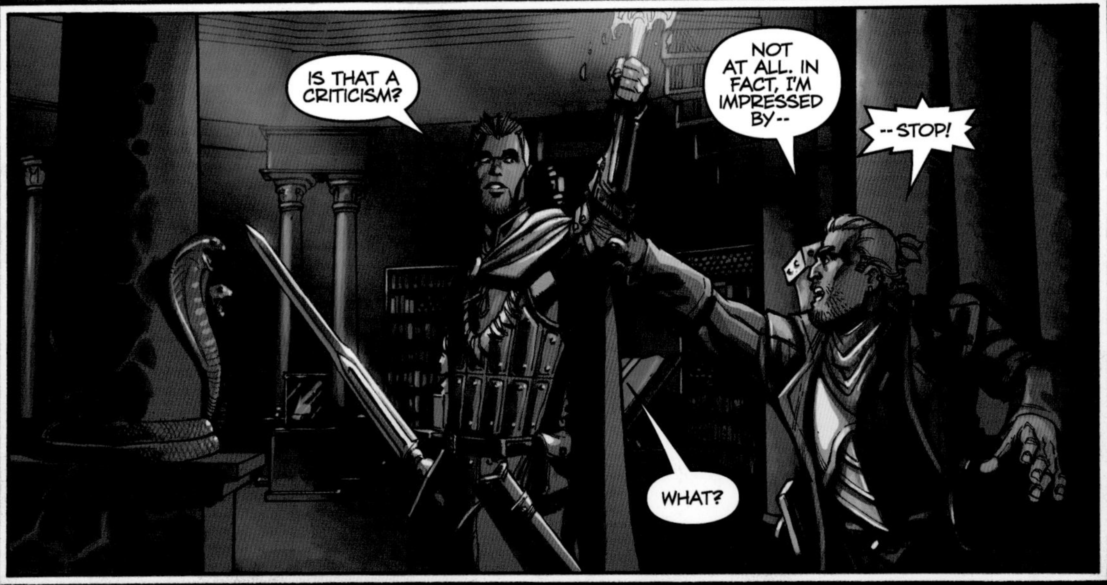
IS THAT A CRITICISM?
NOT AT ALL. IN FACT, I'M IMPRESSED BY --
-- STOP!
WHAT?

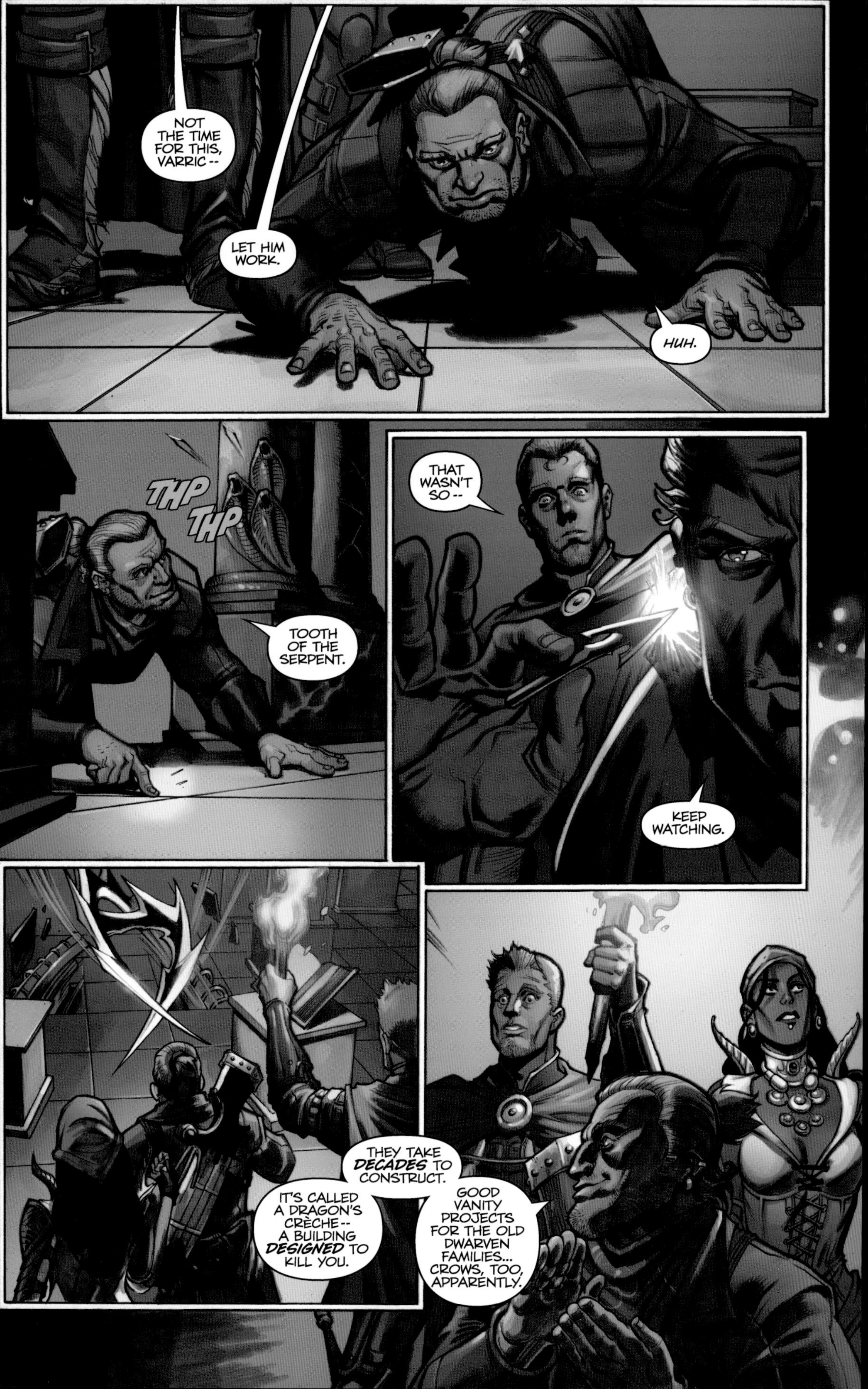
NOT THE TIME FOR THIS, VARRIC --
LET HIM WORK.
HUH.
THP
THP
TOOTH OF THE SERPENT.
THAT WASN'T SO --
KEEP WATCHING.
THEY TAKE *DECADES* TO CONSTRUCT.
IT'S CALLED A DRAGON'S CRÈCHE -- A BUILDING *DESIGNED* TO KILL YOU.
GOOD VANITY PROJECTS FOR THE OLD DWARVEN FAMILIES... CROWS, TOO, APPARENTLY.

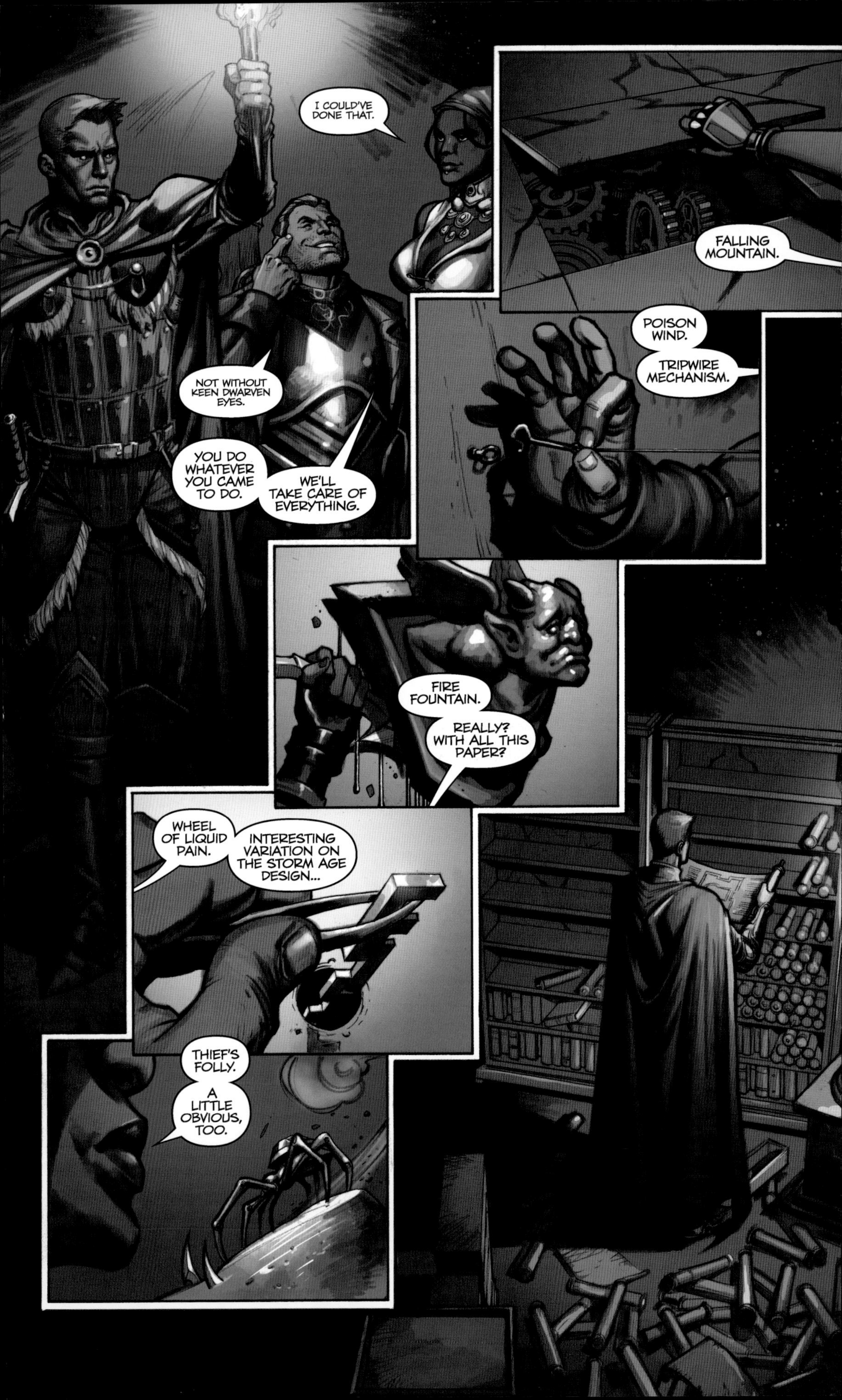
I COULD'VE DONE THAT.
NOT WITHOUT KEEN DWARVEN EYES.
YOU DO WHATEVER YOU CAME TO DO.
WE'LL TAKE CARE OF EVERYTHING.
FALLING MOUNTAIN.
POISON WIND.
TRIPWIRE MECHANISM.
FIRE FOUNTAIN.
REALLY? WITH ALL THIS PAPER?
WHEEL OF LIQUID PAIN.
INTERESTING VARIATION ON THE STORM AGE DESIGN...
THIEF'S FOLLY.
A LITTLE OBVIOUS, TOO.

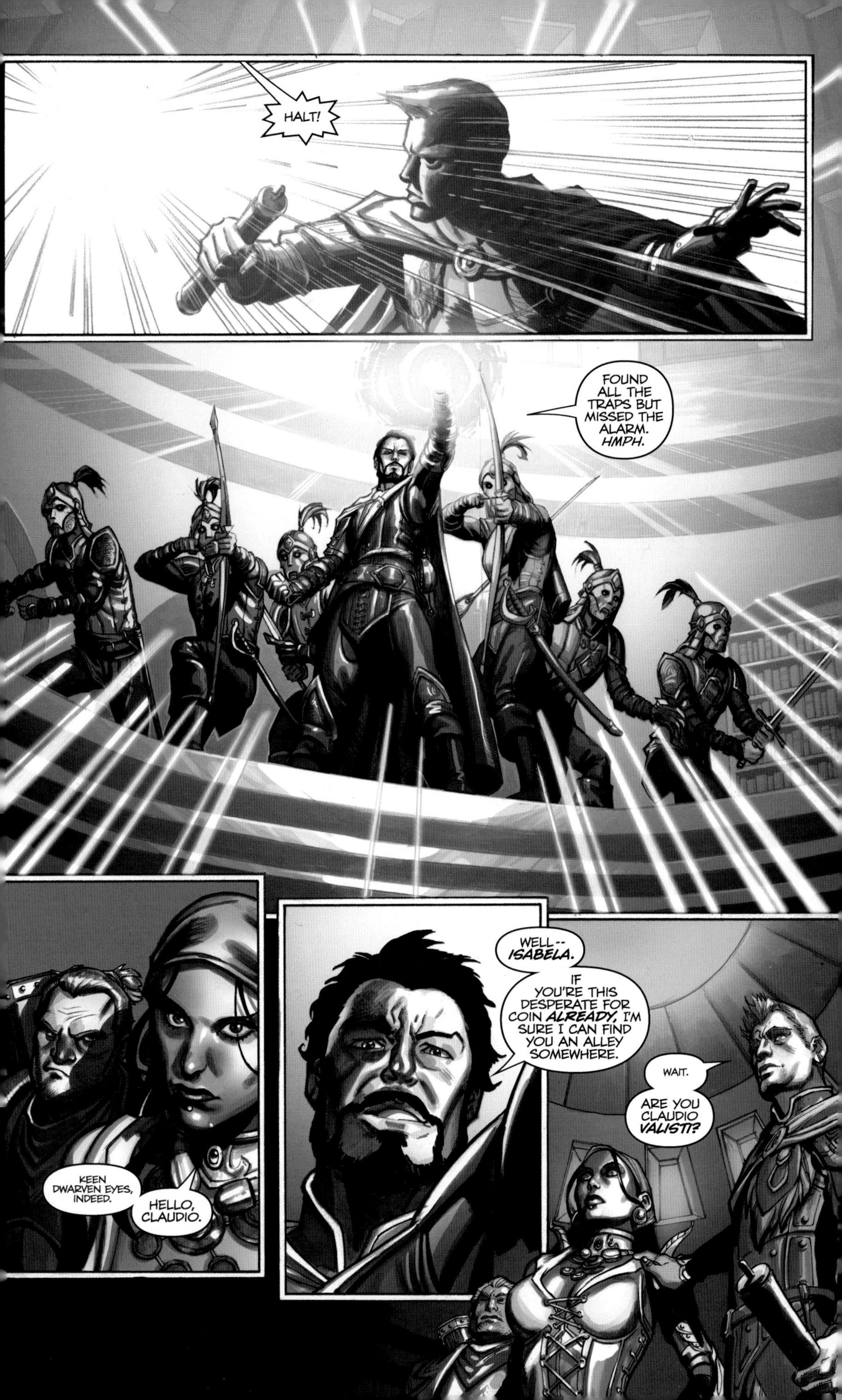
HALT!
FOUND ALL THE TRAPS BUT MISSED THE ALARM. HMPH.
KEEN DWARVEN EYES, INDEED.
HELLO, CLAUDIO.
WELL-- ISABELA.
IF YOU'RE THIS DESPERATE FOR COIN ALREADY, I'M SURE I CAN FIND YOU AN ALLEY SOMEWHERE.
WAIT.
ARE YOU CLAUDIO VALISTI?

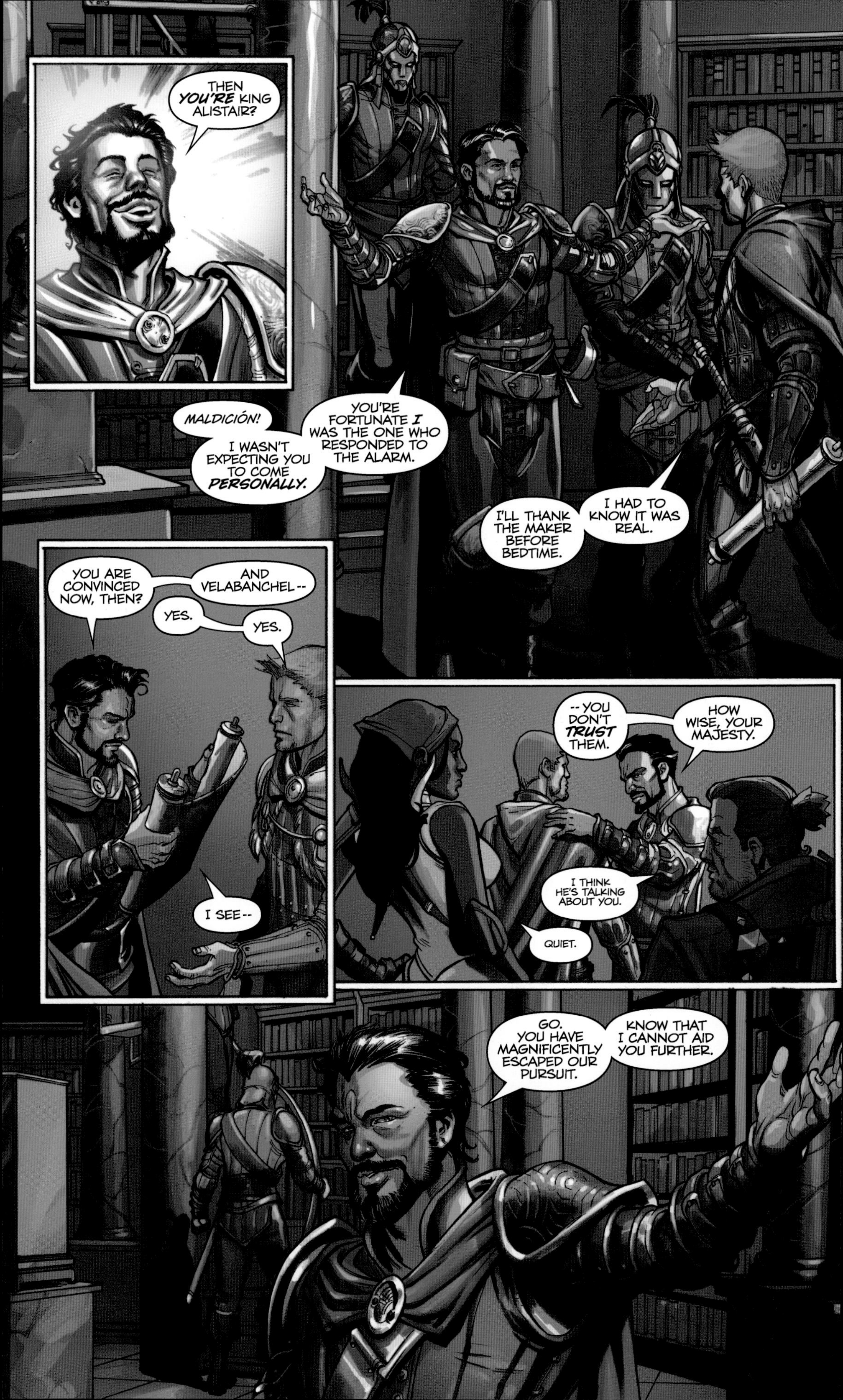
THEN *YOU'RE* KING ALISTAIR?
MALDICIÓN!
I WASN'T EXPECTING YOU TO COME ***PERSONALLY.***
YOU'RE FORTUNATE *I* WAS THE ONE WHO RESPONDED TO THE ALARM.
I HAD TO KNOW IT WAS REAL.
I'LL THANK THE MAKER BEFORE BEDTIME.
YOU ARE CONVINCED NOW, THEN?
AND VELABANCHEL --
YES.
YES.
I SEE --
-- YOU DON'T ***TRUST*** THEM.
HOW WISE, YOUR MAJESTY.
I THINK HE'S TALKING ABOUT YOU.
QUIET.
GO. YOU HAVE MAGNIFICENTLY ESCAPED OUR PURSUIT.
KNOW THAT I CANNOT AID YOU FURTHER.

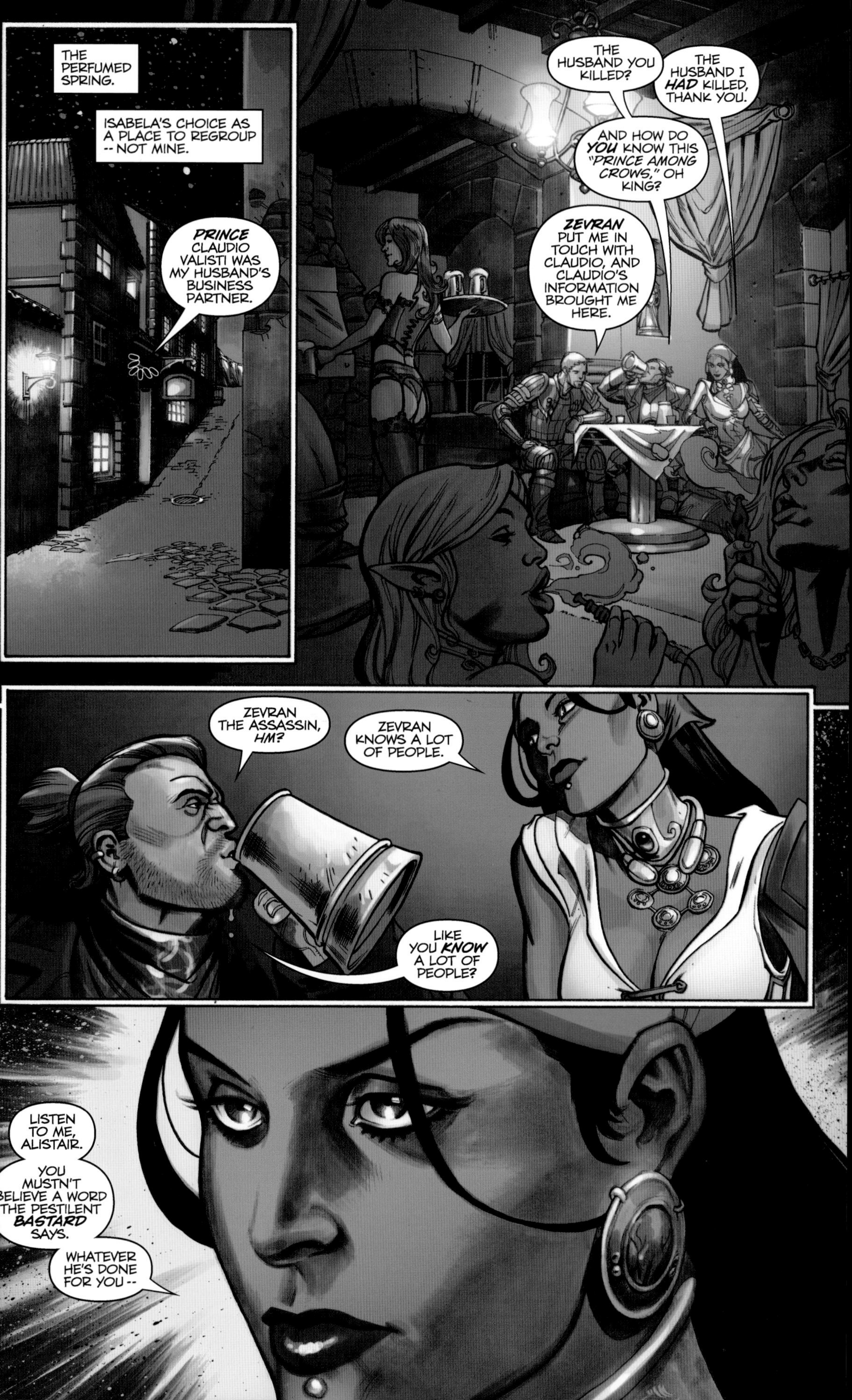
THE PERFUMED SPRING.
ISABELA'S CHOICE AS A PLACE TO REGROUP -- NOT MINE.
PRINCE CLAUDIO VALISTI WAS MY HUSBAND'S BUSINESS PARTNER.
THE HUSBAND YOU KILLED?
THE HUSBAND I HAD KILLED, THANK YOU.
AND HOW DO YOU KNOW THIS "PRINCE AMONG CROWS," OH KING?
ZEVRAN PUT ME IN TOUCH WITH CLAUDIO, AND CLAUDIO'S INFORMATION BROUGHT ME HERE.
ZEVRAN THE ASSASSIN, HM?
ZEVRAN KNOWS A LOT OF PEOPLE.
LIKE YOU KNOW A LOT OF PEOPLE?
LISTEN TO ME, ALISTAIR.
YOU MUSTN'T BELIEVE A WORD THE PESTILENT BASTARD SAYS.
WHATEVER HE'S DONE FOR YOU --

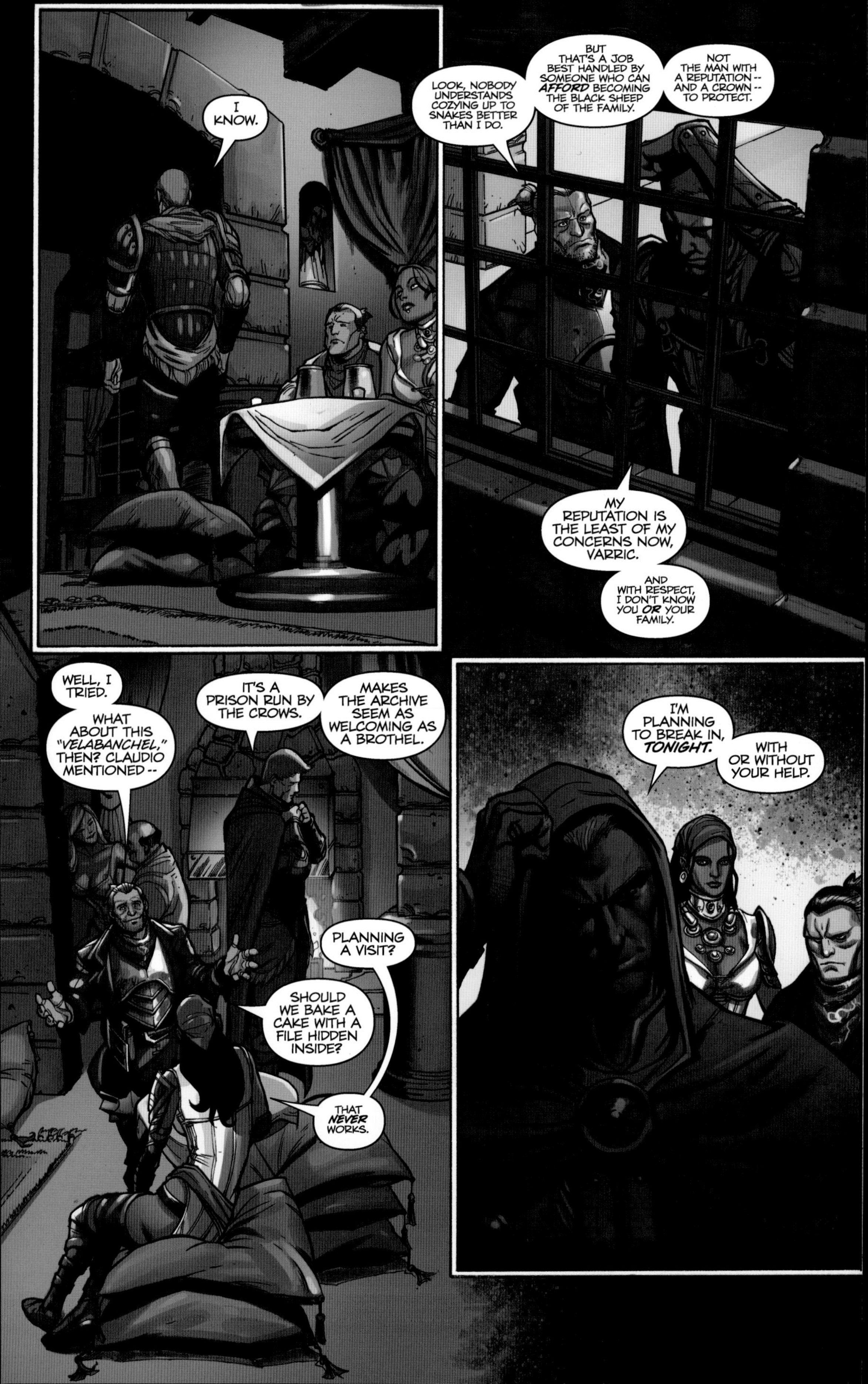
I KNOW.
LOOK, NOBODY UNDERSTANDS COZYING UP TO SNAKES BETTER THAN I DO.
BUT THAT'S A JOB BEST HANDLED BY SOMEONE WHO CAN AFFORD BECOMING THE BLACK SHEEP OF THE FAMILY.
NOT THE MAN WITH A REPUTATION -- AND A CROWN -- TO PROTECT.
MY REPUTATION IS THE LEAST OF MY CONCERNS NOW, VARRIC.
AND WITH RESPECT, I DON'T KNOW YOU OR YOUR FAMILY.
WELL, I TRIED.
WHAT ABOUT THIS "VELABANCHEL," THEN? CLAUDIO MENTIONED --
IT'S A PRISON RUN BY THE CROWS.
MAKES THE ARCHIVE SEEM AS WELCOMING AS A BROTHEL.
PLANNING A VISIT?
SHOULD WE BAKE A CAKE WITH A FILE HIDDEN INSIDE?
THAT NEVER WORKS.
I'M PLANNING TO BREAK IN, TONIGHT.
WITH OR WITHOUT YOUR HELP.

CHAPTER 2

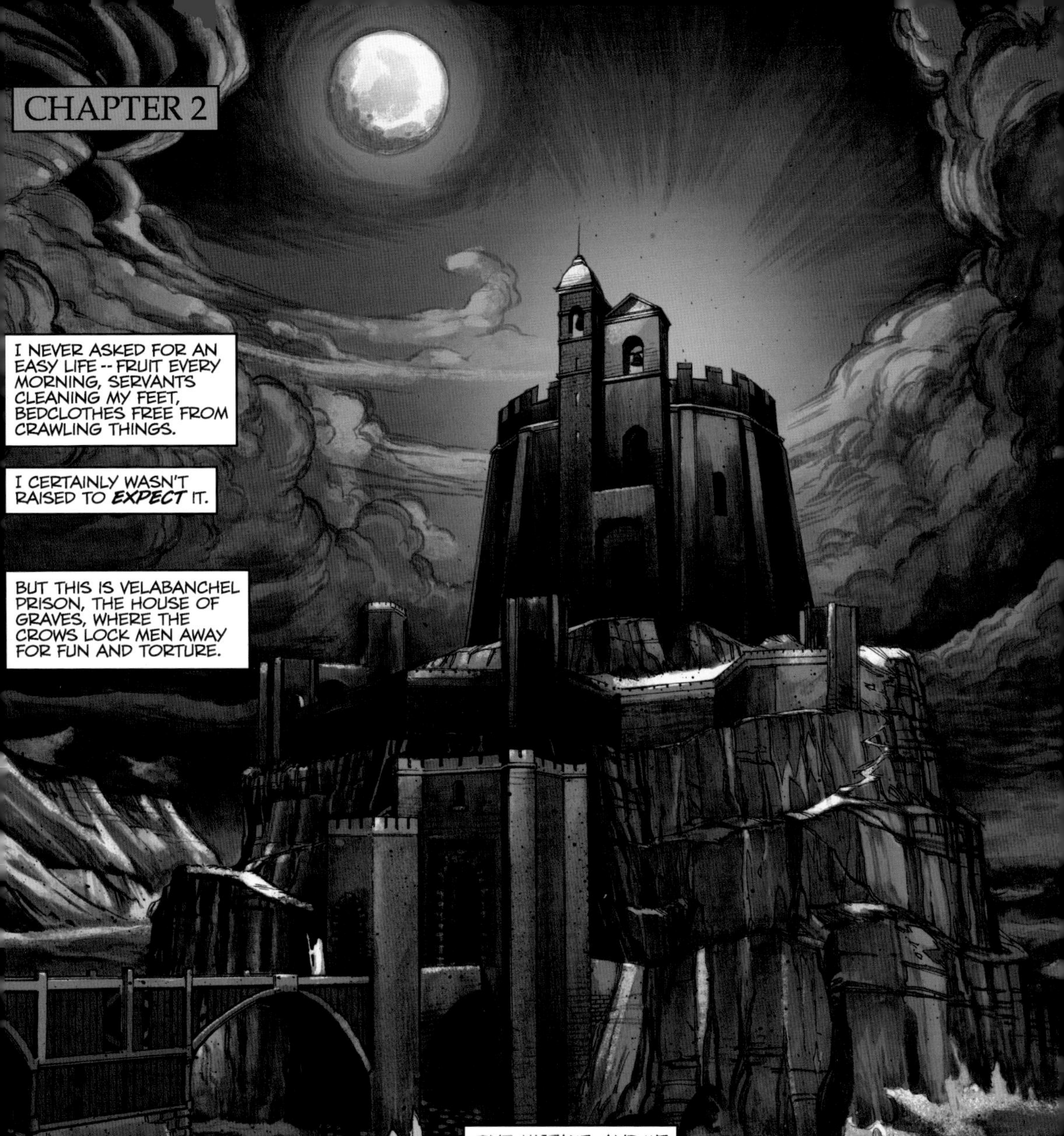

I NEVER ASKED FOR AN EASY LIFE -- FRUIT EVERY MORNING, SERVANTS CLEANING MY FEET, BEDCLOTHES FREE FROM CRAWLING THINGS.
I CERTAINLY WASN'T RAISED TO *EXPECT* IT.
BUT THIS IS VELABANCHEL PRISON, THE HOUSE OF GRAVES, WHERE THE CROWS LOCK MEN AWAY FOR FUN AND TORTURE.
ONE MISTAKE, AND WE SPEND THE REST OF OUR DAYS SHACKLED AND FORGOTTEN IN CELLS BUILT BY LONG-DEAD SADISTS.
FOR THE FIRST TIME, I'M STARTING TO MISS THE ROYAL PALACE.

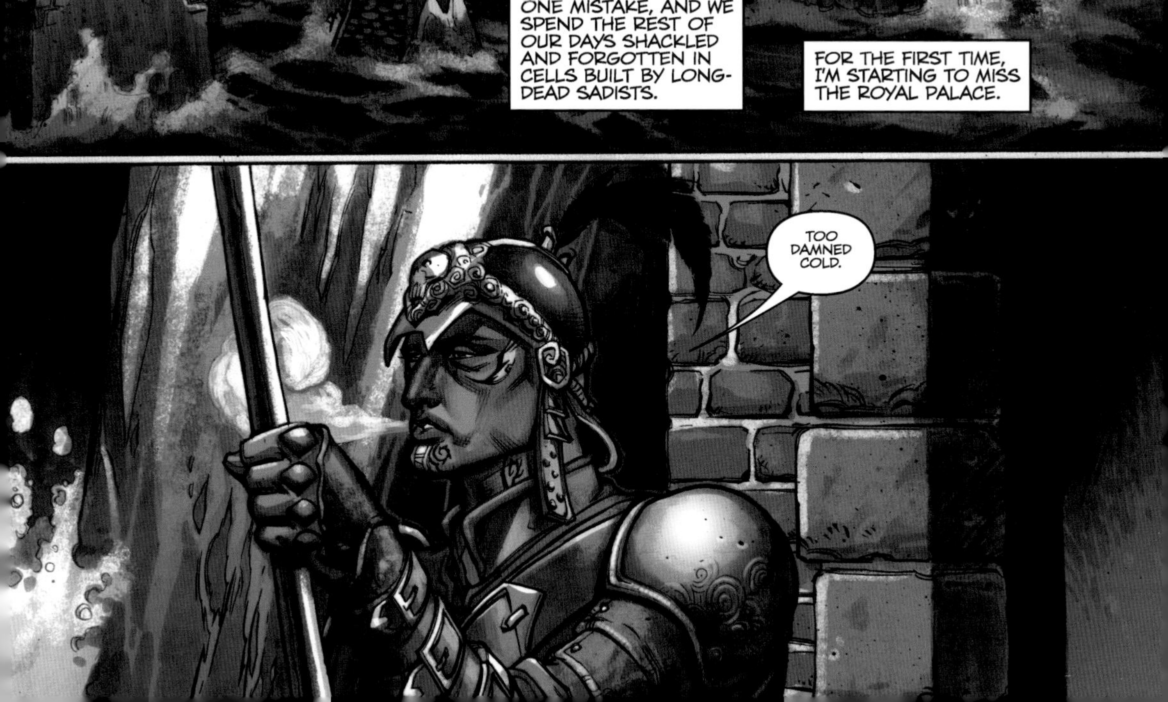

TOO DAMNED COLD.

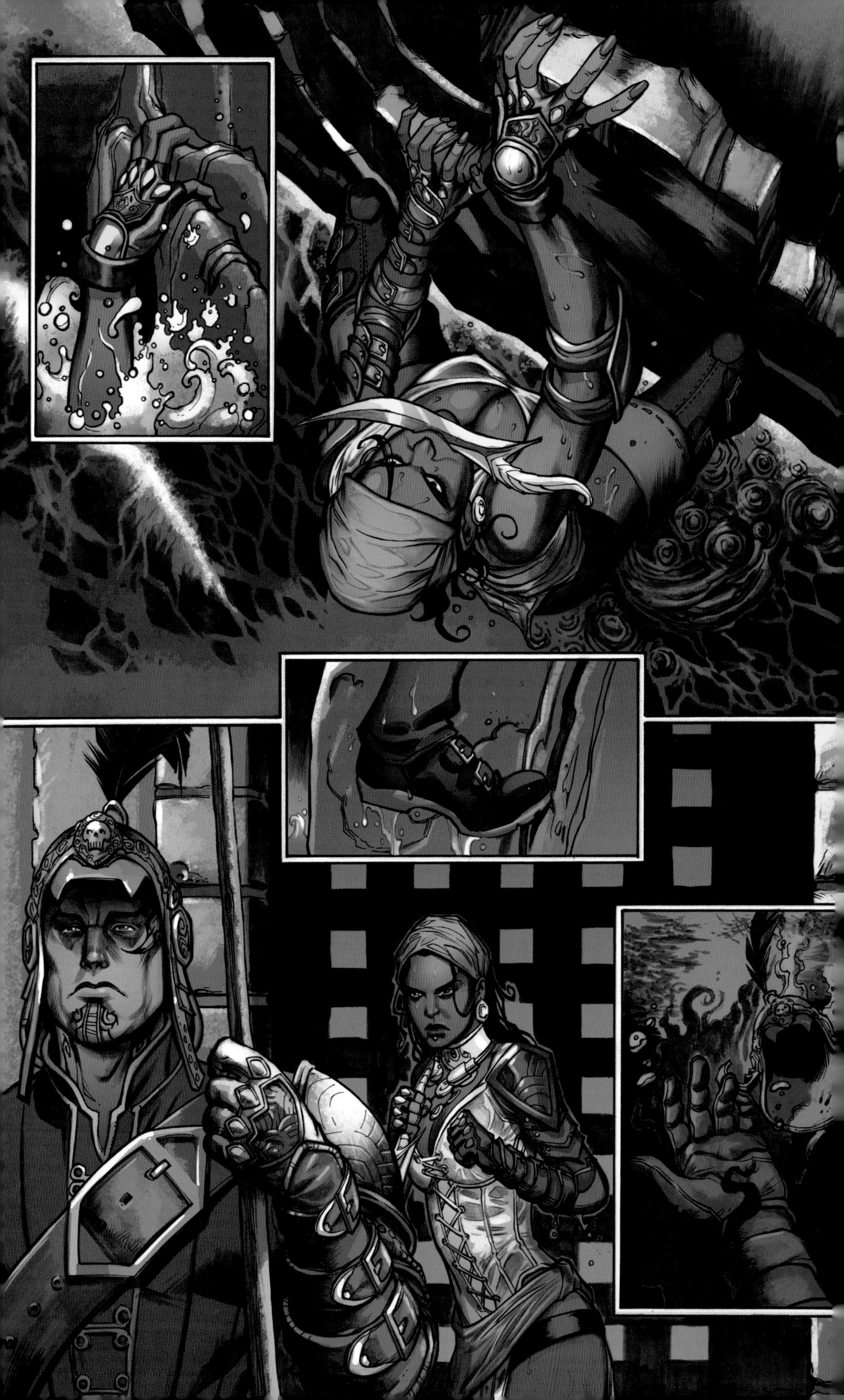

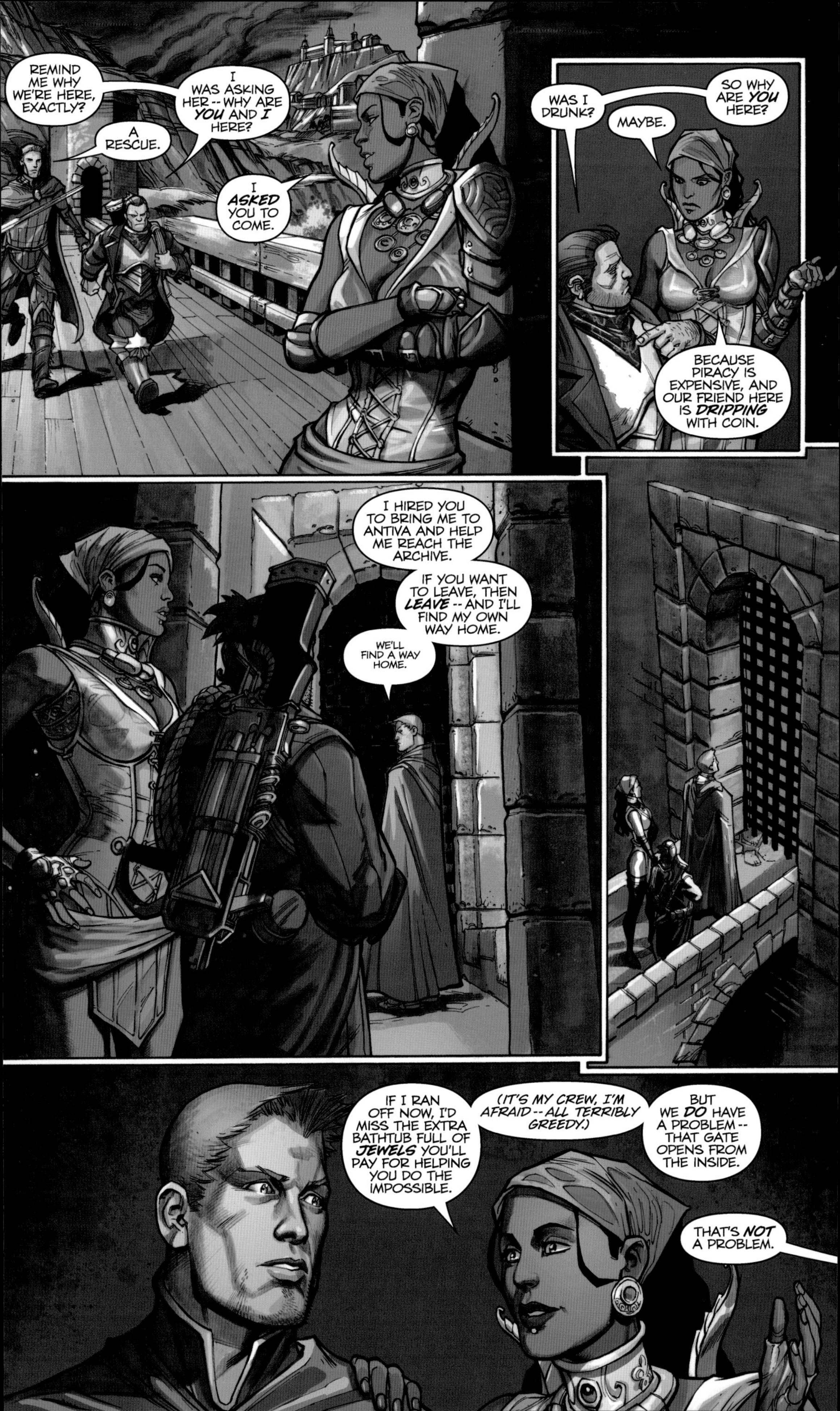
REMIND ME WHY WE'RE HERE, EXACTLY?
I WAS ASKING HER -- WHY ARE YOU AND I HERE?
A RESCUE.
I ASKED YOU TO COME.
WAS I DRUNK?
SO WHY ARE YOU HERE?
MAYBE.
BECAUSE PIRACY IS EXPENSIVE, AND OUR FRIEND HERE IS DRIPPING WITH COIN.
I HIRED YOU TO BRING ME TO ANTIVA AND HELP ME REACH THE ARCHIVE.
IF YOU WANT TO LEAVE, THEN LEAVE -- AND I'LL FIND MY OWN WAY HOME.
WE'LL FIND A WAY HOME.
IF I RAN OFF NOW, I'D MISS THE EXTRA BATHTUB FULL OF JEWELS YOU'LL PAY FOR HELPING YOU DO THE IMPOSSIBLE.
(IT'S MY CREW, I'M AFRAID -- ALL TERRIBLY GREEDY.)
BUT WE DO HAVE A PROBLEM -- THAT GATE OPENS FROM THE INSIDE.
THAT'S NOT A PROBLEM.

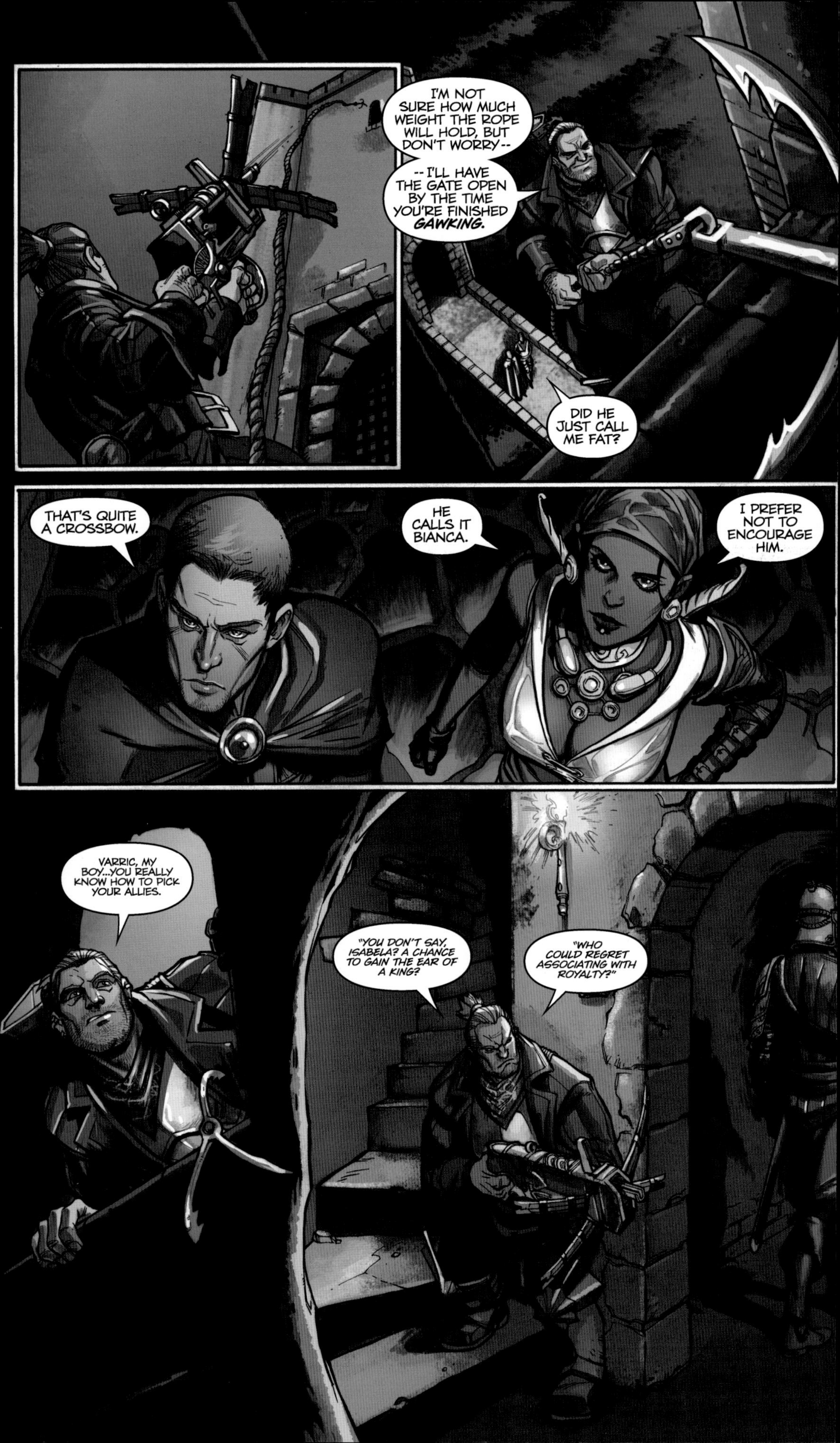
I'M NOT SURE HOW MUCH WEIGHT THE ROPE WILL HOLD, BUT DON'T WORRY--
--I'LL HAVE THE GATE OPEN BY THE TIME YOU'RE FINISHED ***GAWKING.***
DID HE JUST CALL ME FAT?
THAT'S QUITE A CROSSBOW.
HE CALLS IT BIANCA.
I PREFER NOT TO ENCOURAGE HIM.
VARRIC, MY BOY...YOU REALLY KNOW HOW TO PICK YOUR ALLIES.
"YOU DON'T SAY, ISABELA? A CHANCE TO GAIN THE EAR OF A KING?
"WHO COULD REGRET ASSOCIATING WITH ROYALTY?"

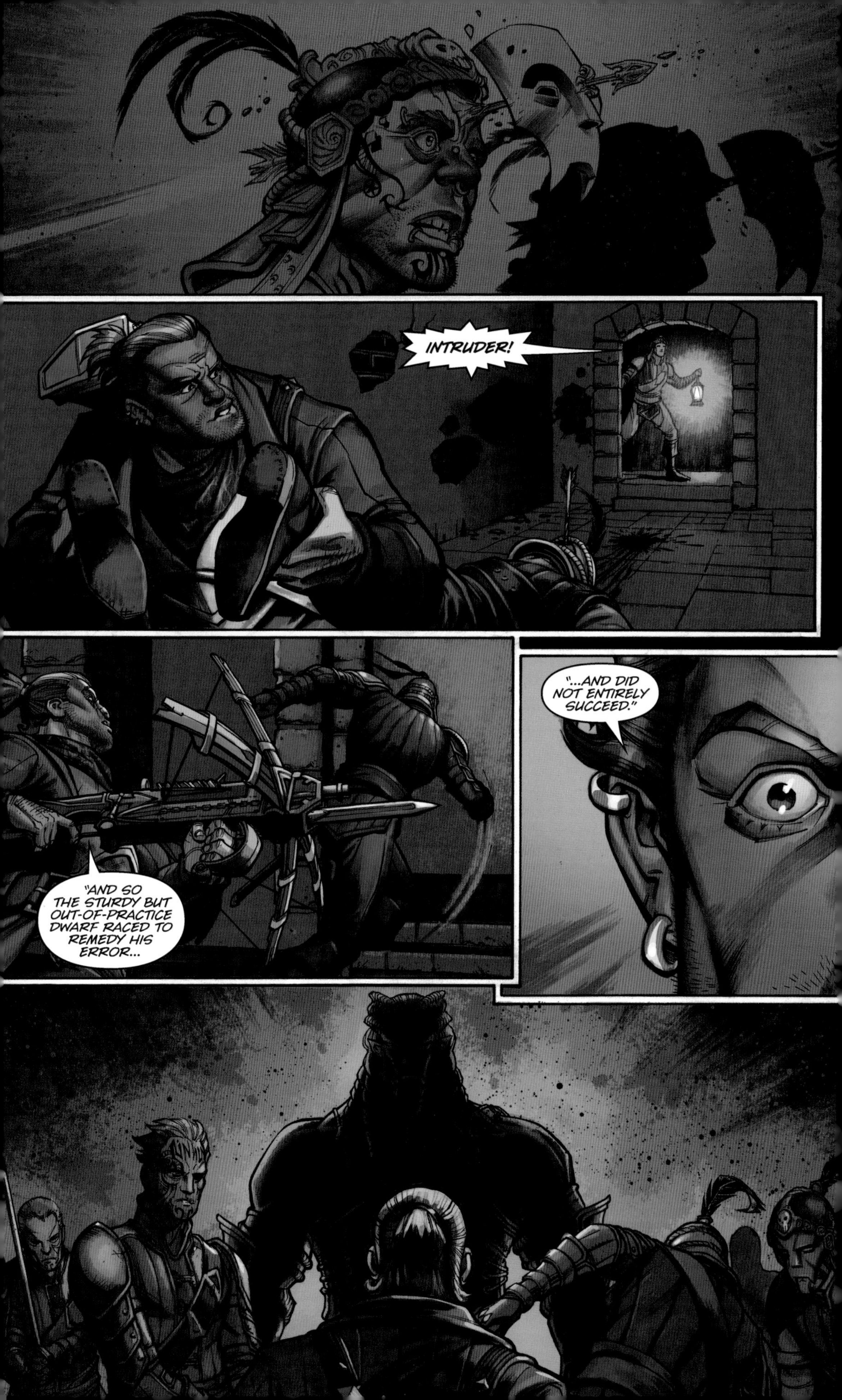
INTRUDER!
"AND SO THE STURDY BUT OUT-OF-PRACTICE DWARF RACED TO REMEDY HIS ERROR...
"...AND DID NOT ENTIRELY SUCCEED."

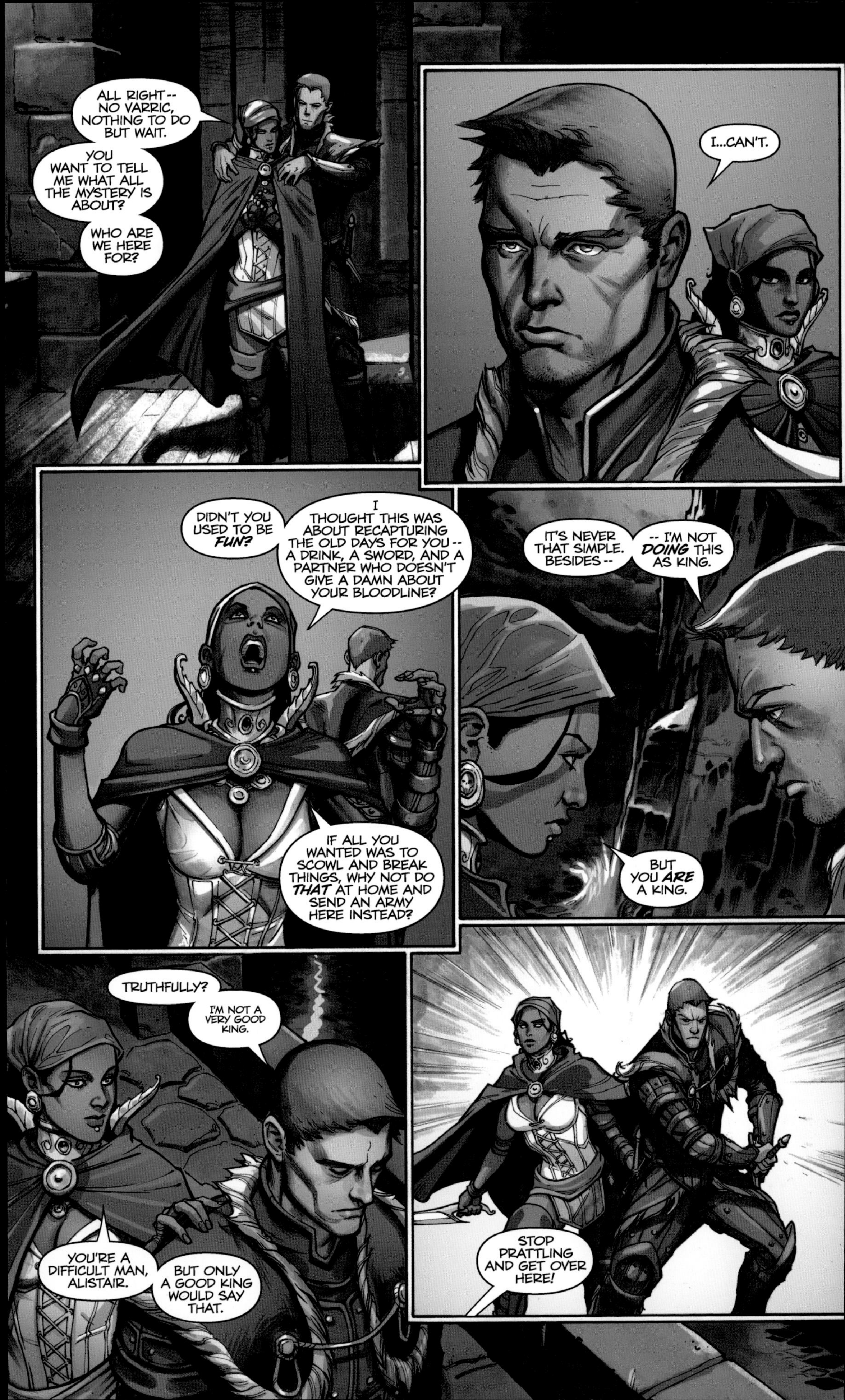
ALL RIGHT -- NO VARRIC, NOTHING TO DO BUT WAIT.
YOU WANT TO TELL ME WHAT ALL THE MYSTERY IS ABOUT?
WHO ARE WE HERE FOR?
I...CAN'T.
DIDN'T YOU USED TO BE *FUN?*
I THOUGHT THIS WAS ABOUT RECAPTURING THE OLD DAYS FOR YOU -- A DRINK, A SWORD, AND A PARTNER WHO DOESN'T GIVE A DAMN ABOUT YOUR BLOODLINE?
IF ALL YOU WANTED WAS TO SCOWL AND BREAK THINGS, WHY NOT DO *THAT* AT HOME AND SEND AN ARMY HERE INSTEAD?
IT'S NEVER THAT SIMPLE. BESIDES --
-- I'M NOT *DOING* THIS AS KING.
BUT YOU *ARE* A KING.
TRUTHFULLY?
I'M NOT A VERY GOOD KING.
YOU'RE A DIFFICULT MAN, ALISTAIR.
BUT ONLY A GOOD KING WOULD SAY THAT.
STOP PRATTLING AND GET OVER HERE!

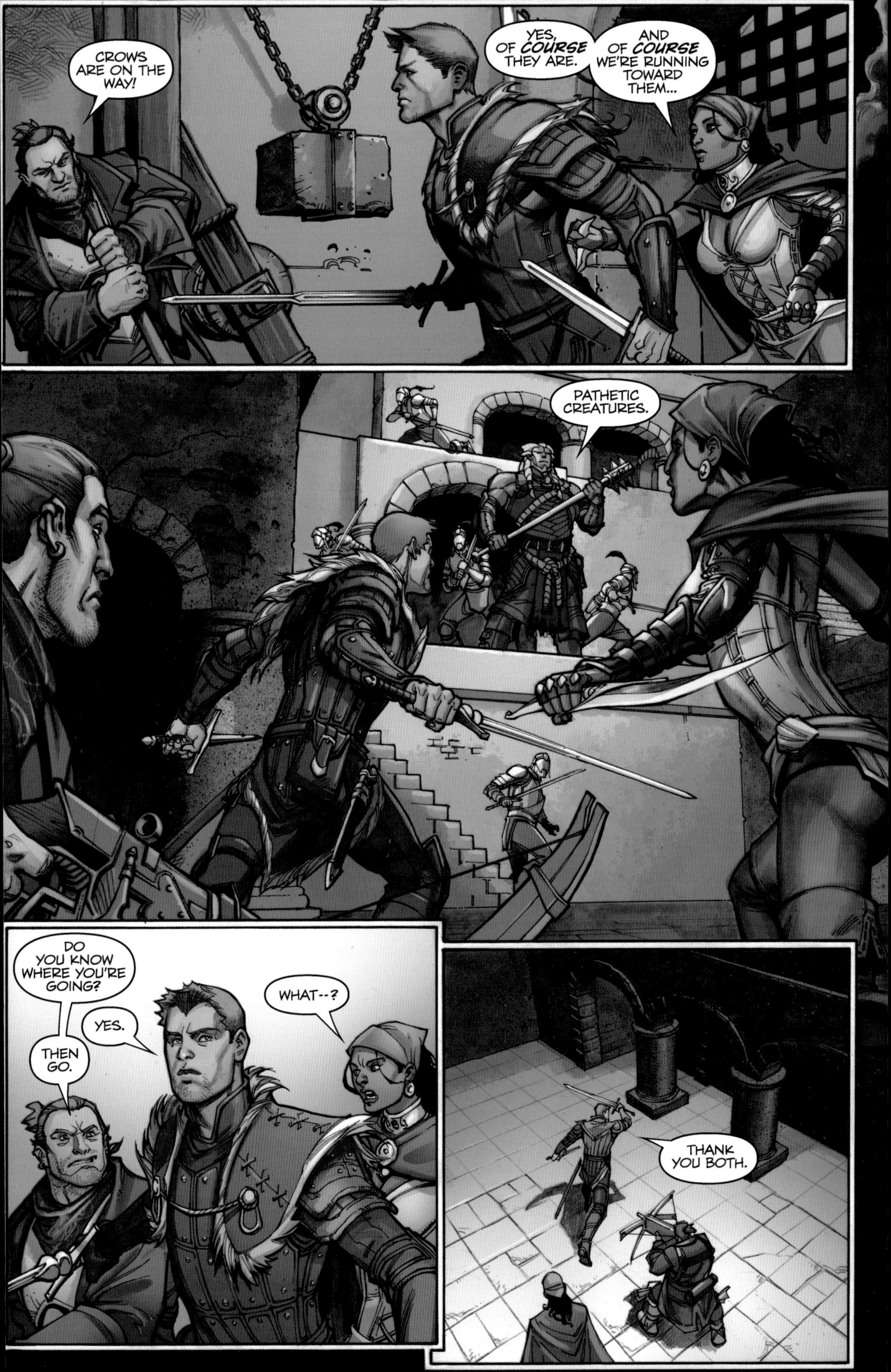
CROWS ARE ON THE WAY!
YES, OF COURSE THEY ARE.
AND OF COURSE WE'RE RUNNING TOWARD THEM...
PATHETIC CREATURES.
DO YOU KNOW WHERE YOU'RE GOING?
YES.
THEN GO.
WHAT--?
THANK YOU BOTH.

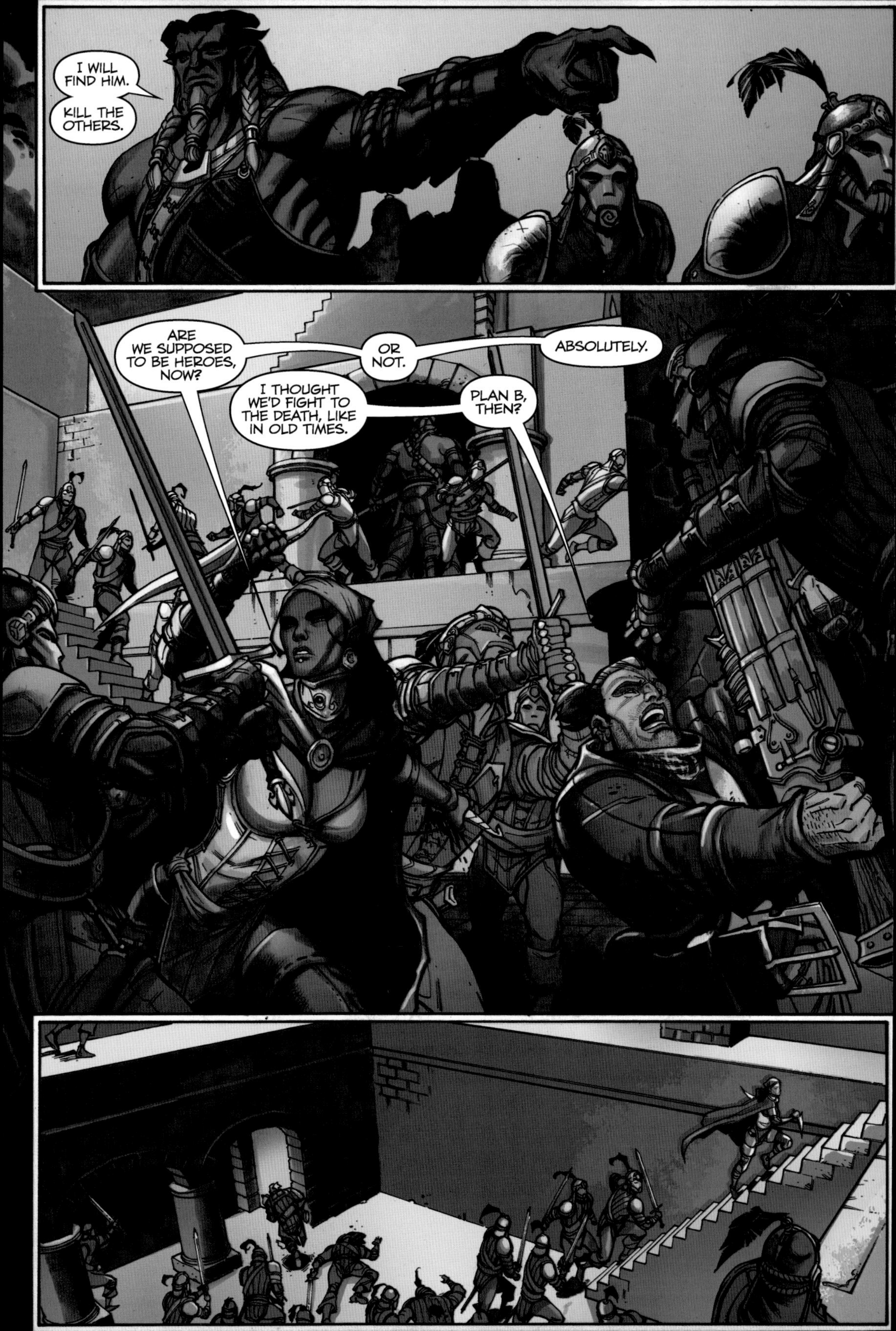
I WILL FIND HIM.
KILL THE OTHERS.
ARE WE SUPPOSED TO BE HEROES, NOW?
OR NOT.
ABSOLUTELY.
I THOUGHT WE'D FIGHT TO THE DEATH, LIKE IN OLD TIMES.
PLAN B, THEN?

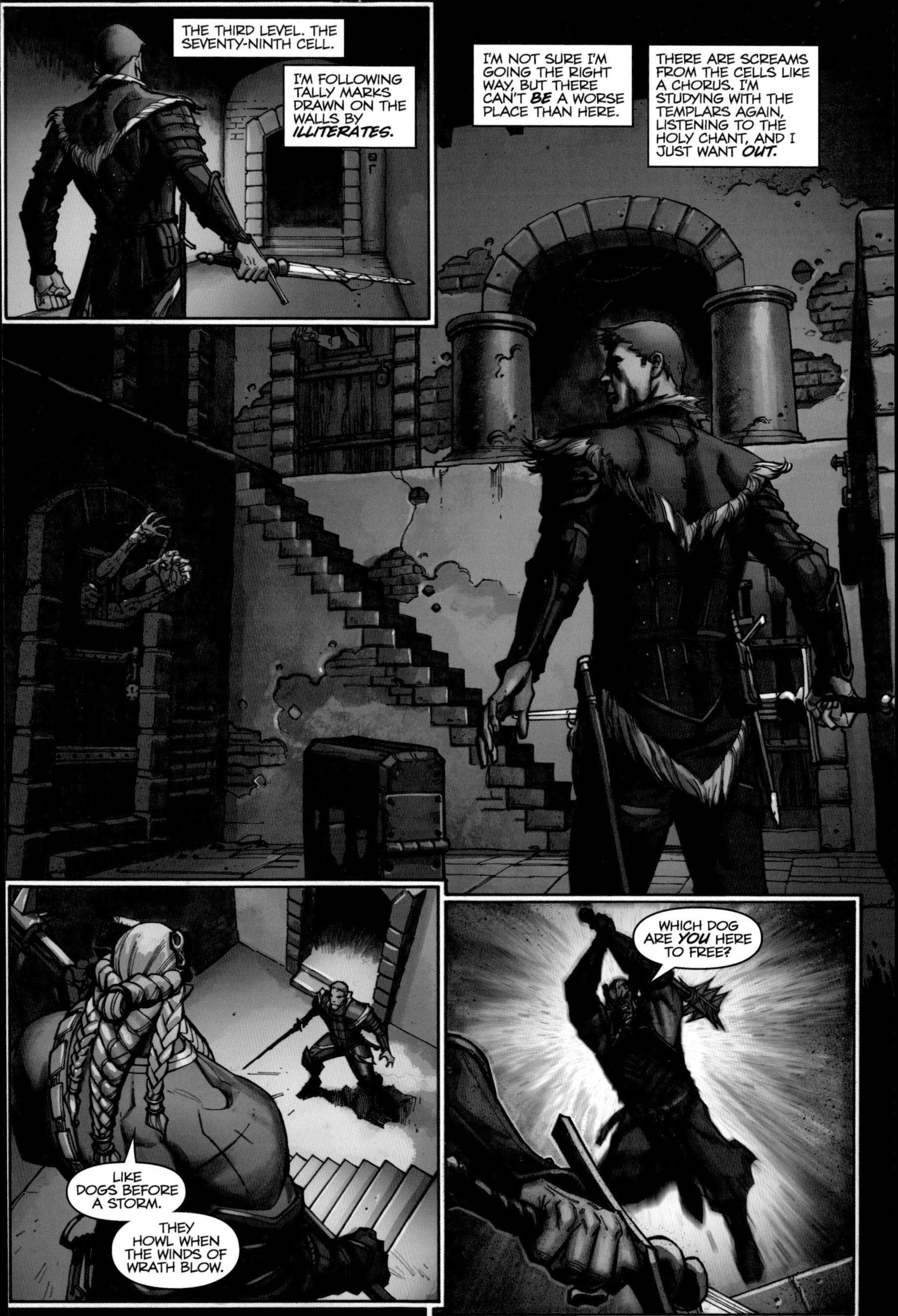
THE THIRD LEVEL. THE SEVENTY-NINTH CELL.
I'M FOLLOWING TALLY MARKS DRAWN ON THE WALLS BY ILLITERATES.
I'M NOT SURE I'M GOING THE RIGHT WAY, BUT THERE CAN'T BE A WORSE PLACE THAN HERE.
THERE ARE SCREAMS FROM THE CELLS LIKE A CHORUS. I'M STUDYING WITH THE TEMPLARS AGAIN, LISTENING TO THE HOLY CHANT, AND I JUST WANT OUT.
LIKE DOGS BEFORE A STORM.
THEY HOWL WHEN THE WINDS OF WRATH BLOW.
WHICH DOG ARE YOU HERE TO FREE?

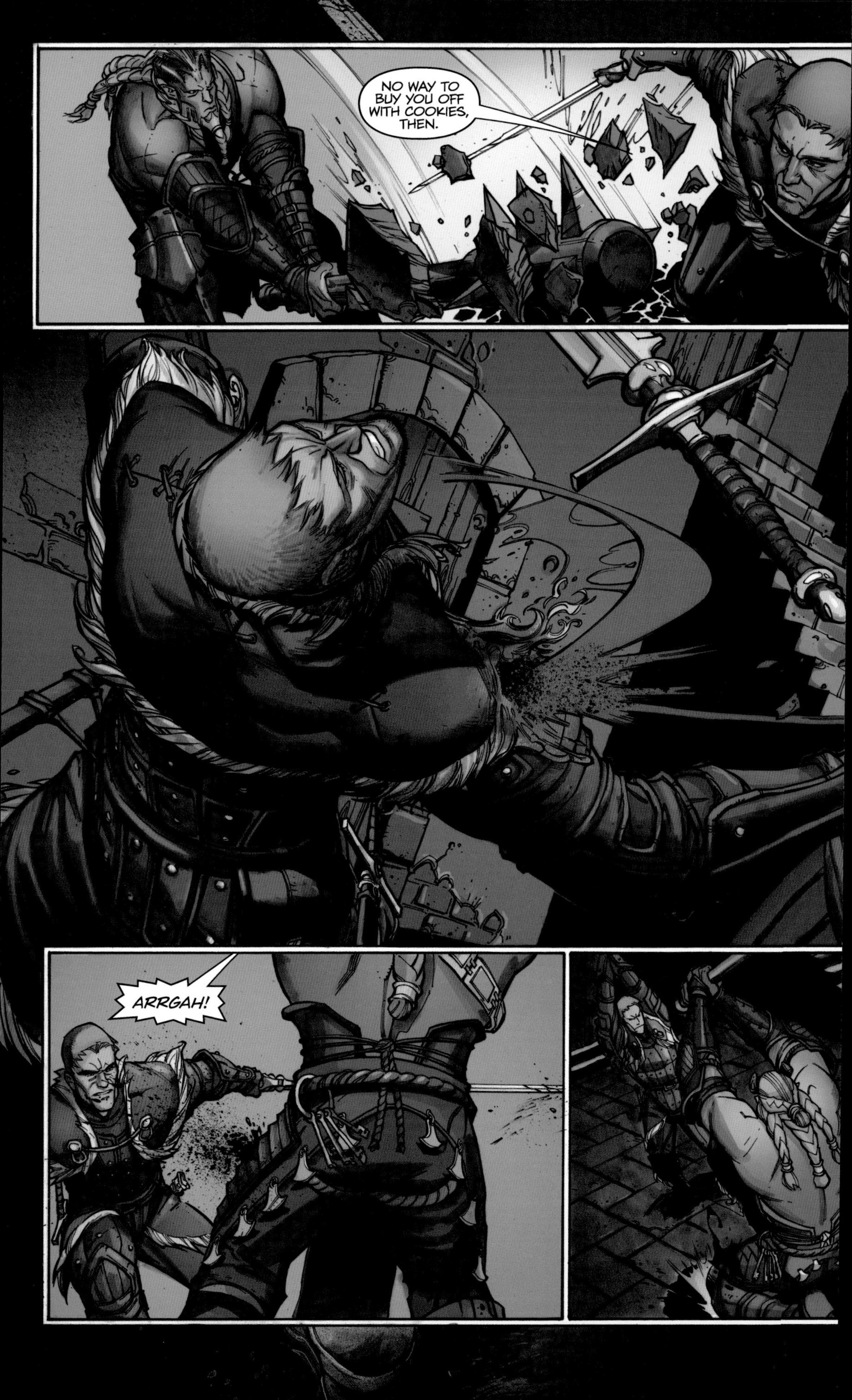
NO WAY TO BUY YOU OFF WITH COOKIES, THEN.
ARRGAH!

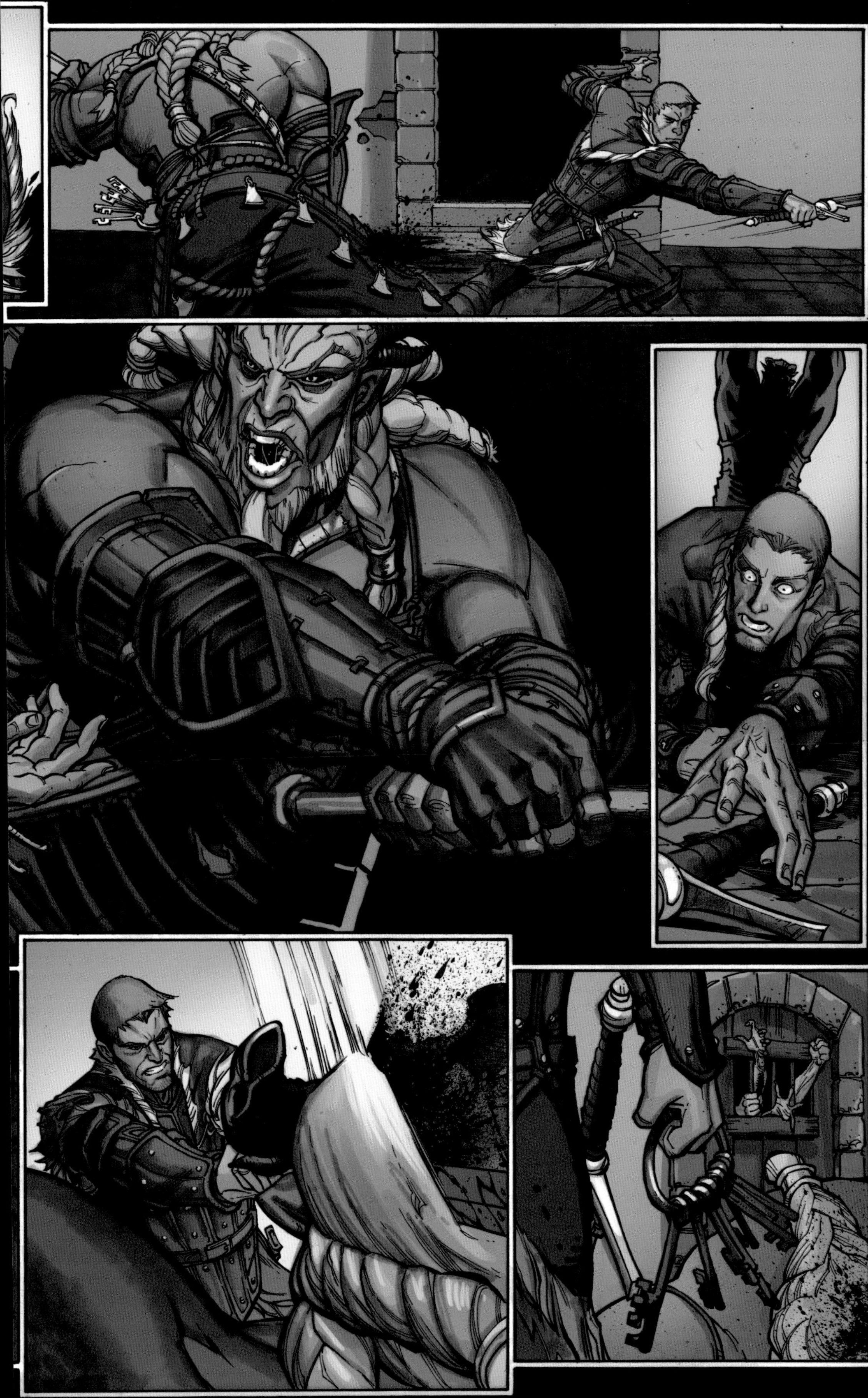

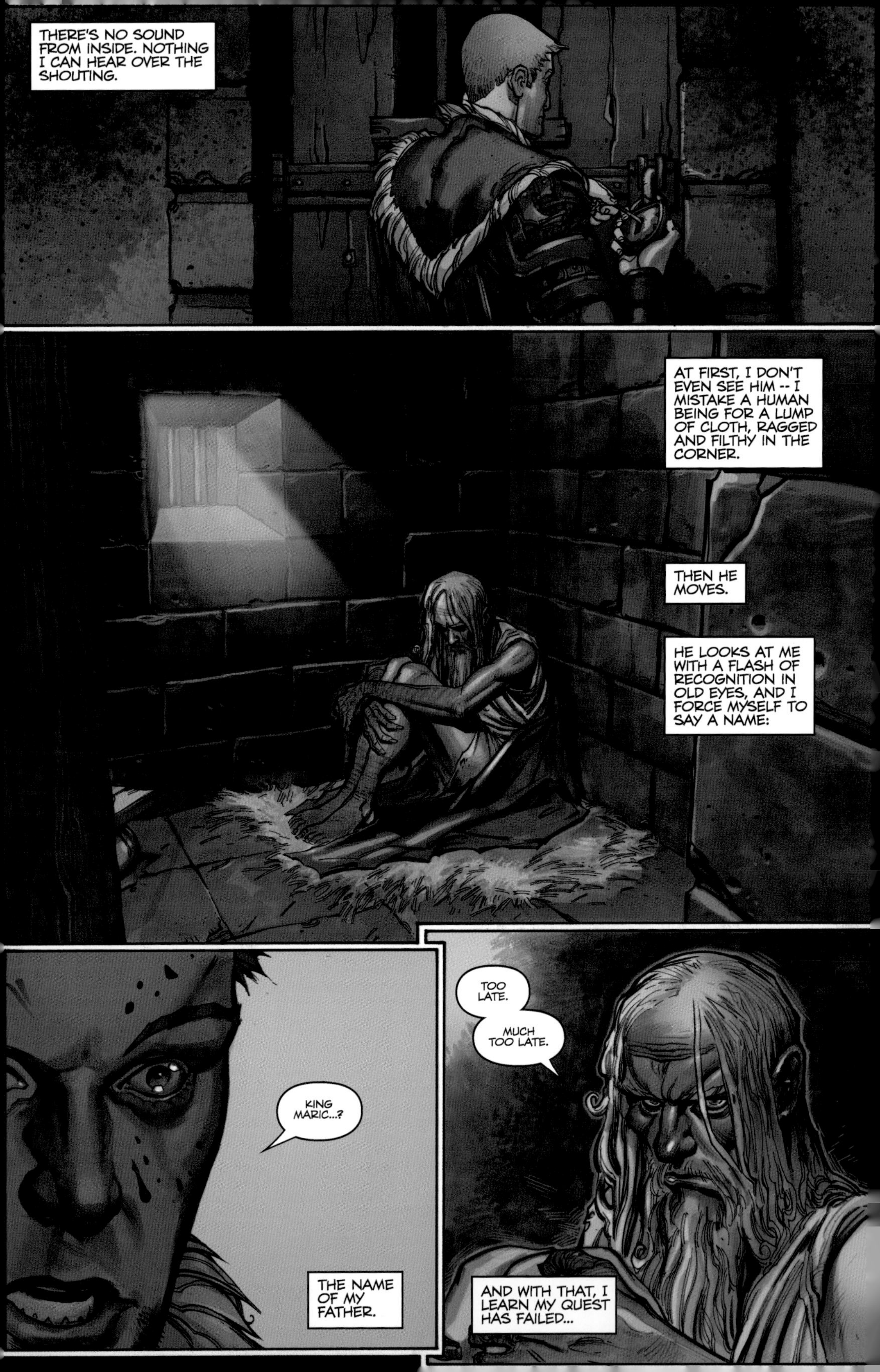
THERE'S NO SOUND FROM INSIDE. NOTHING I CAN HEAR OVER THE SHOUTING.
AT FIRST, I DON'T EVEN SEE HIM -- I MISTAKE A HUMAN BEING FOR A LUMP OF CLOTH, RAGGED AND FILTHY IN THE CORNER.
THEN HE MOVES.
HE LOOKS AT ME WITH A FLASH OF RECOGNITION IN OLD EYES, AND I FORCE MYSELF TO SAY A NAME:
KING MARIC...?
THE NAME OF MY FATHER.
TOO LATE.
MUCH TOO LATE.
AND WITH THAT, I LEARN MY QUEST HAS FAILED...

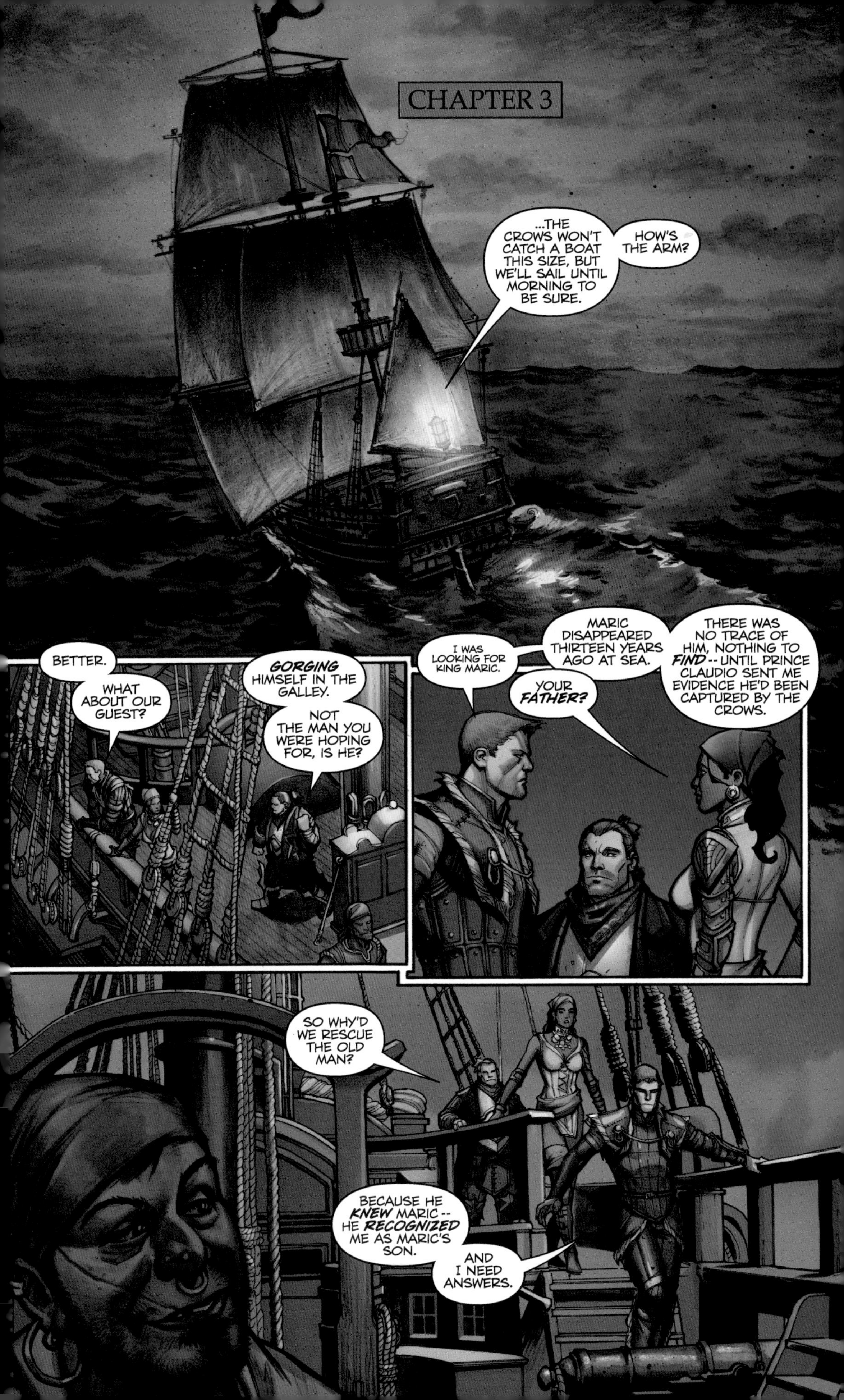
CHAPTER 3
...THE CROWS WON'T CATCH A BOAT THIS SIZE, BUT WE'LL SAIL UNTIL MORNING TO BE SURE.
HOW'S THE ARM?
BETTER.
WHAT ABOUT OUR GUEST?
GORGING HIMSELF IN THE GALLEY.
NOT THE MAN YOU WERE HOPING FOR, IS HE?
I WAS LOOKING FOR KING MARIC.
YOUR FATHER?
MARIC DISAPPEARED THIRTEEN YEARS AGO AT SEA.
THERE WAS NO TRACE OF HIM, NOTHING TO FIND -- UNTIL PRINCE CLAUDIO SENT ME EVIDENCE HE'D BEEN CAPTURED BY THE CROWS.
SO WHY'D WE RESCUE THE OLD MAN?
BECAUSE HE KNEW MARIC -- HE RECOGNIZED ME AS MARIC'S SON.
AND I NEED ANSWERS.

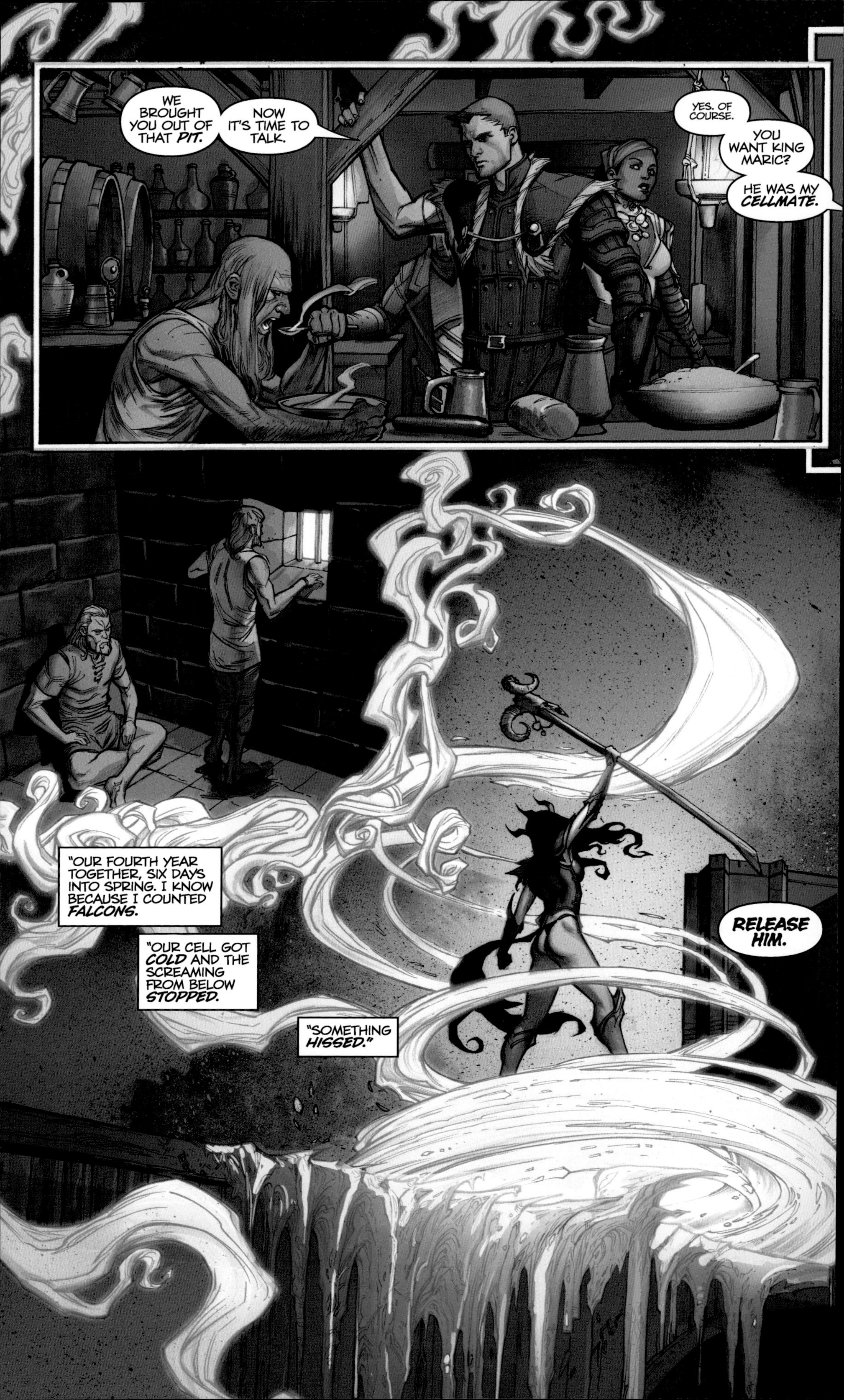
WE BROUGHT YOU OUT OF THAT PIT.
NOW IT'S TIME TO TALK.
YES. OF COURSE.
YOU WANT KING MARIC?
HE WAS MY CELLMATE.
"OUR FOURTH YEAR TOGETHER, SIX DAYS INTO SPRING. I KNOW BECAUSE I COUNTED FALCONS.
"OUR CELL GOT COLD AND THE SCREAMING FROM BELOW STOPPED.
"SOMETHING HISSED."
RELEASE HIM.

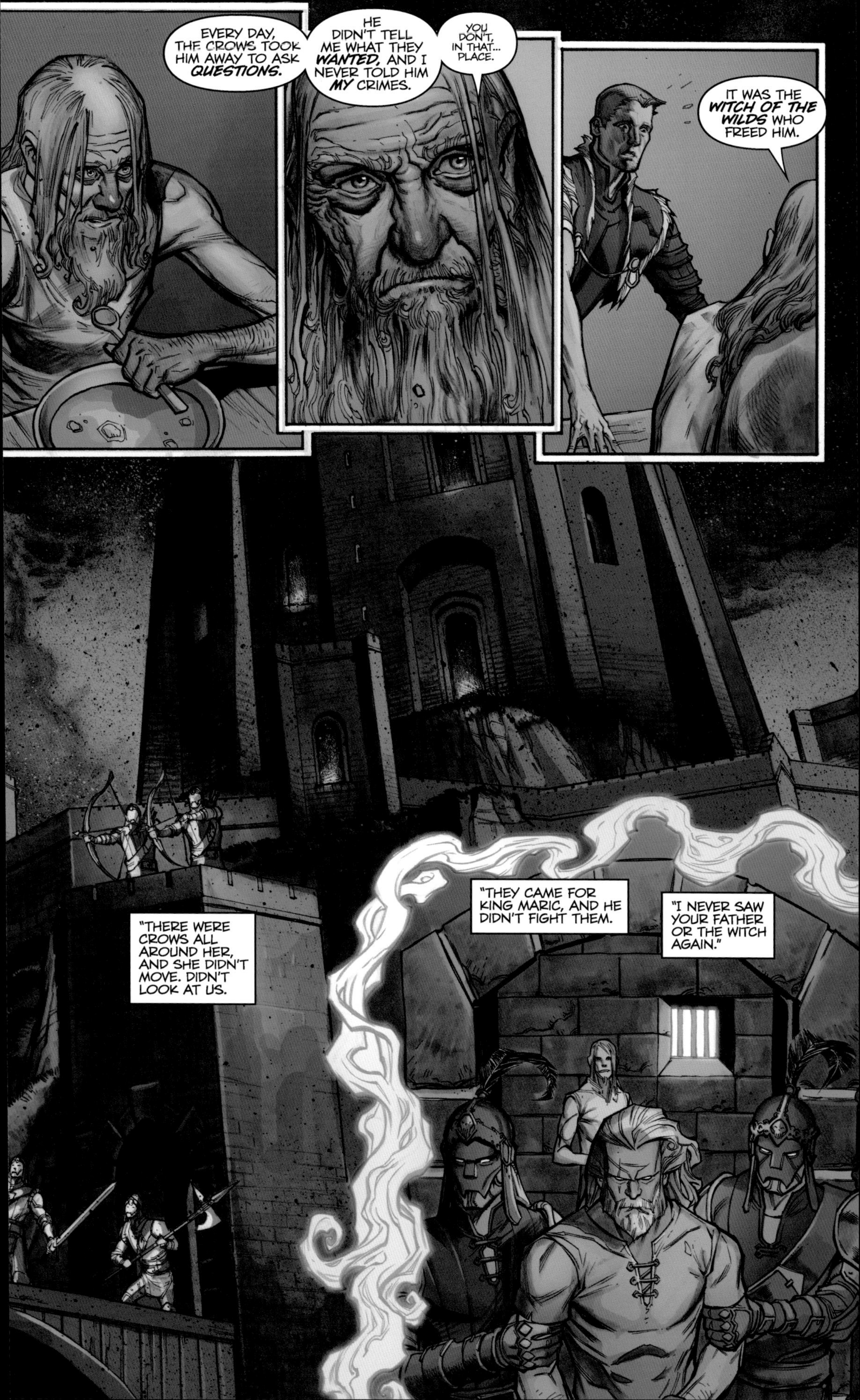
EVERY DAY, THE CROWS TOOK HIM AWAY TO ASK QUESTIONS.
HE DIDN'T TELL ME WHAT THEY WANTED, AND I NEVER TOLD HIM MY CRIMES.
YOU DON'T, IN THAT... PLACE.
IT WAS THE WITCH OF THE WILDS WHO FREED HIM.
"THERE WERE CROWS ALL AROUND HER, AND SHE DIDN'T MOVE. DIDN'T LOOK AT US.
"THEY CAME FOR KING MARIC, AND HE DIDN'T FIGHT THEM.
"I NEVER SAW YOUR FATHER OR THE WITCH AGAIN."

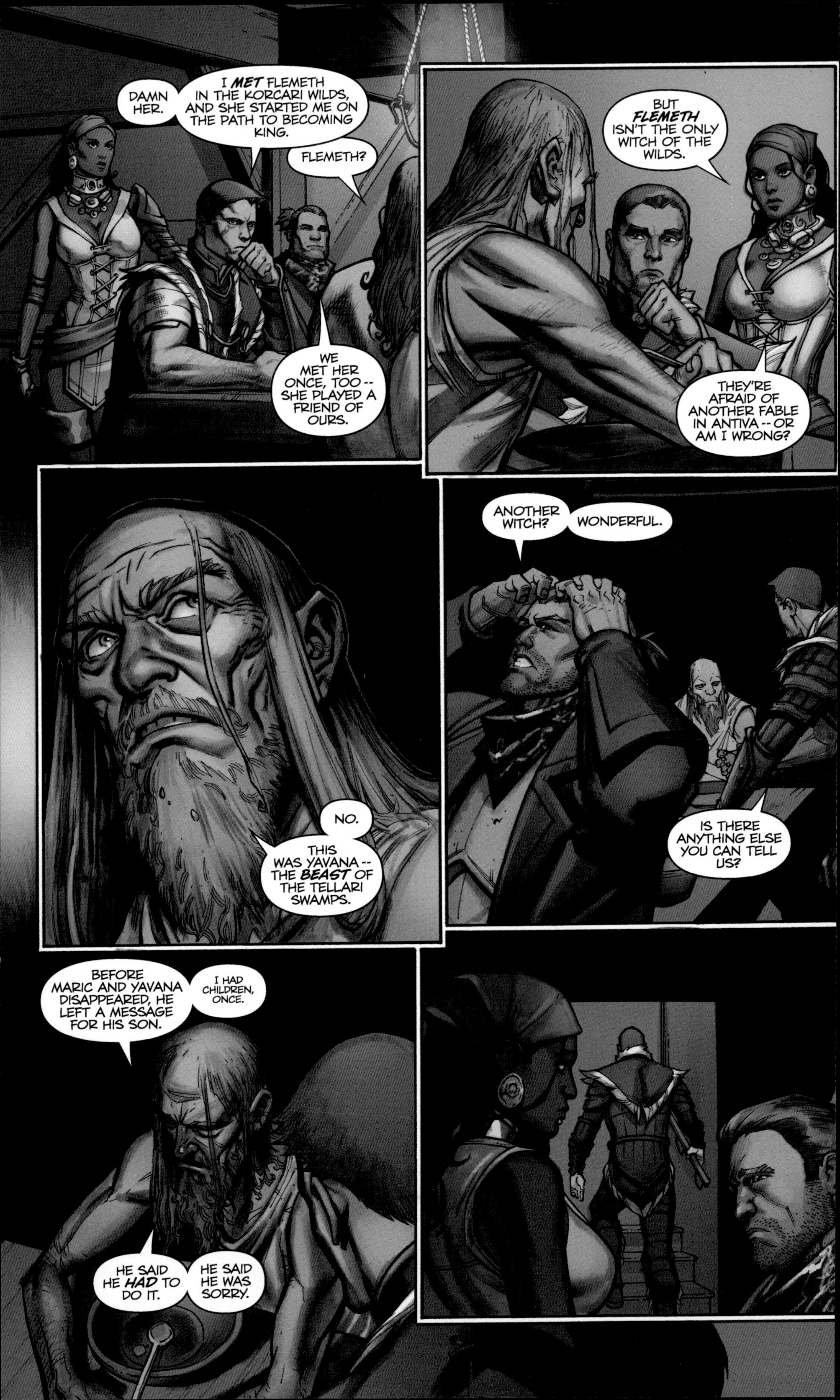
DAMN HER.
I MET FLEMETH IN THE KORCARI WILDS, AND SHE STARTED ME ON THE PATH TO BECOMING KING.
FLEMETH?
WE MET HER ONCE, TOO -- SHE PLAYED A FRIEND OF OURS.
BUT FLEMETH ISN'T THE ONLY WITCH OF THE WILDS.
THEY'RE AFRAID OF ANOTHER FABLE IN ANTIVA -- OR AM I WRONG?
NO.
THIS WAS YAVANA -- THE BEAST OF THE TELLARI SWAMPS.
ANOTHER WITCH?
WONDERFUL.
IS THERE ANYTHING ELSE YOU CAN TELL US?
BEFORE MARIC AND YAVANA DISAPPEARED, HE LEFT A MESSAGE FOR HIS SON.
I HAD CHILDREN, ONCE.
HE SAID HE HAD TO DO IT.
HE SAID HE WAS SORRY.

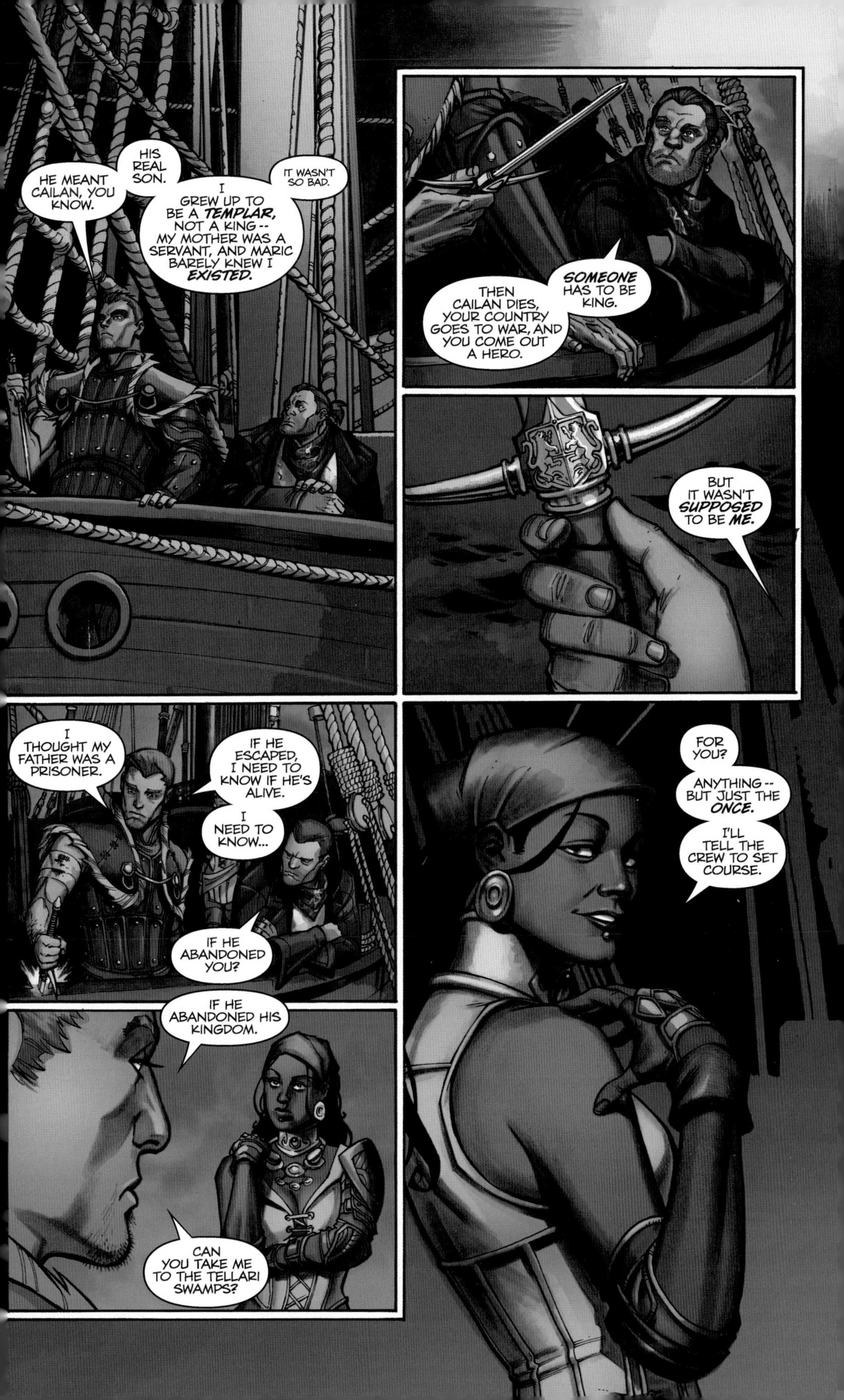

HE MEANT CAILAN, YOU KNOW.
HIS REAL SON.
I GREW UP TO BE A **TEMPLAR,** NOT A KING -- MY MOTHER WAS A SERVANT, AND MARIC BARELY KNEW I **EXISTED.**
IT WASN'T SO BAD.
SOMEONE HAS TO BE KING.
THEN CAILAN DIES, YOUR COUNTRY GOES TO WAR, AND YOU COME OUT A HERO.
BUT IT WASN'T **SUPPOSED** TO BE **ME.**
I THOUGHT MY FATHER WAS A PRISONER.
IF HE ESCAPED, I NEED TO KNOW IF HE'S ALIVE.
I NEED TO KNOW...
IF HE ABANDONED YOU?
IF HE ABANDONED HIS KINGDOM.
CAN YOU TAKE ME TO THE TELLARI SWAMPS?
FOR YOU?
ANYTHING -- BUT JUST THE **ONCE.**
I'LL TELL THE CREW TO SET COURSE.

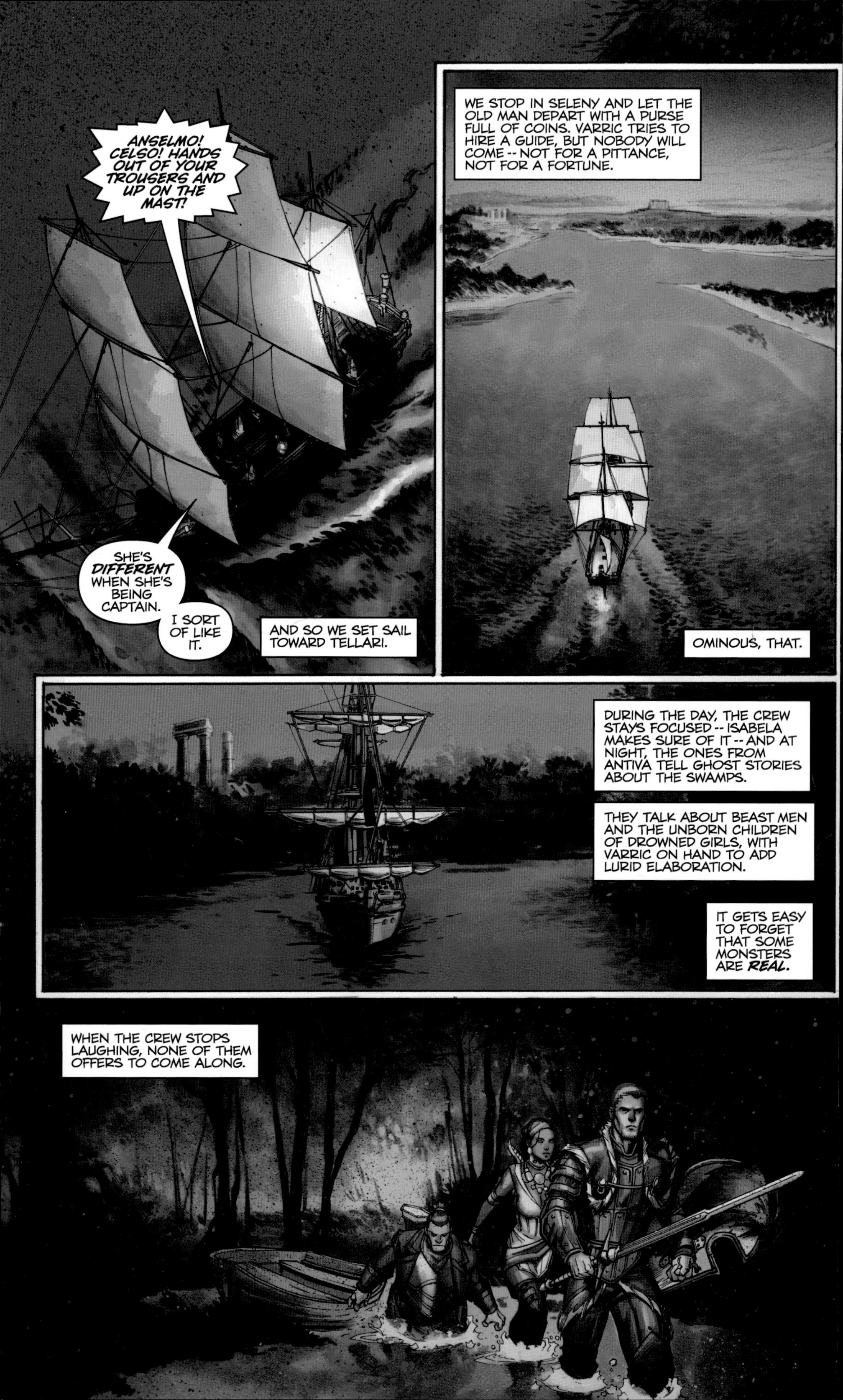
ANSELMO! CELSO! HANDS OUT OF YOUR TROUSERS AND UP ON THE MAST!
SHE'S DIFFERENT WHEN SHE'S BEING CAPTAIN.
I SORT OF LIKE IT.
AND SO WE SET SAIL TOWARD TELLARI.
WE STOP IN SELENY AND LET THE OLD MAN DEPART WITH A PURSE FULL OF COINS. VARRIC TRIES TO HIRE A GUIDE, BUT NOBODY WILL COME -- NOT FOR A PITTANCE, NOT FOR A FORTUNE.
OMINOUS, THAT.
DURING THE DAY, THE CREW STAYS FOCUSED -- ISABELA MAKES SURE OF IT -- AND AT NIGHT, THE ONES FROM ANTIVA TELL GHOST STORIES ABOUT THE SWAMPS.
THEY TALK ABOUT BEAST MEN AND THE UNBORN CHILDREN OF DROWNED GIRLS, WITH VARRIC ON HAND TO ADD LURID ELABORATION.
IT GETS EASY TO FORGET THAT SOME MONSTERS ARE REAL.
WHEN THE CREW STOPS LAUGHING, NONE OF THEM OFFERS TO COME ALONG.

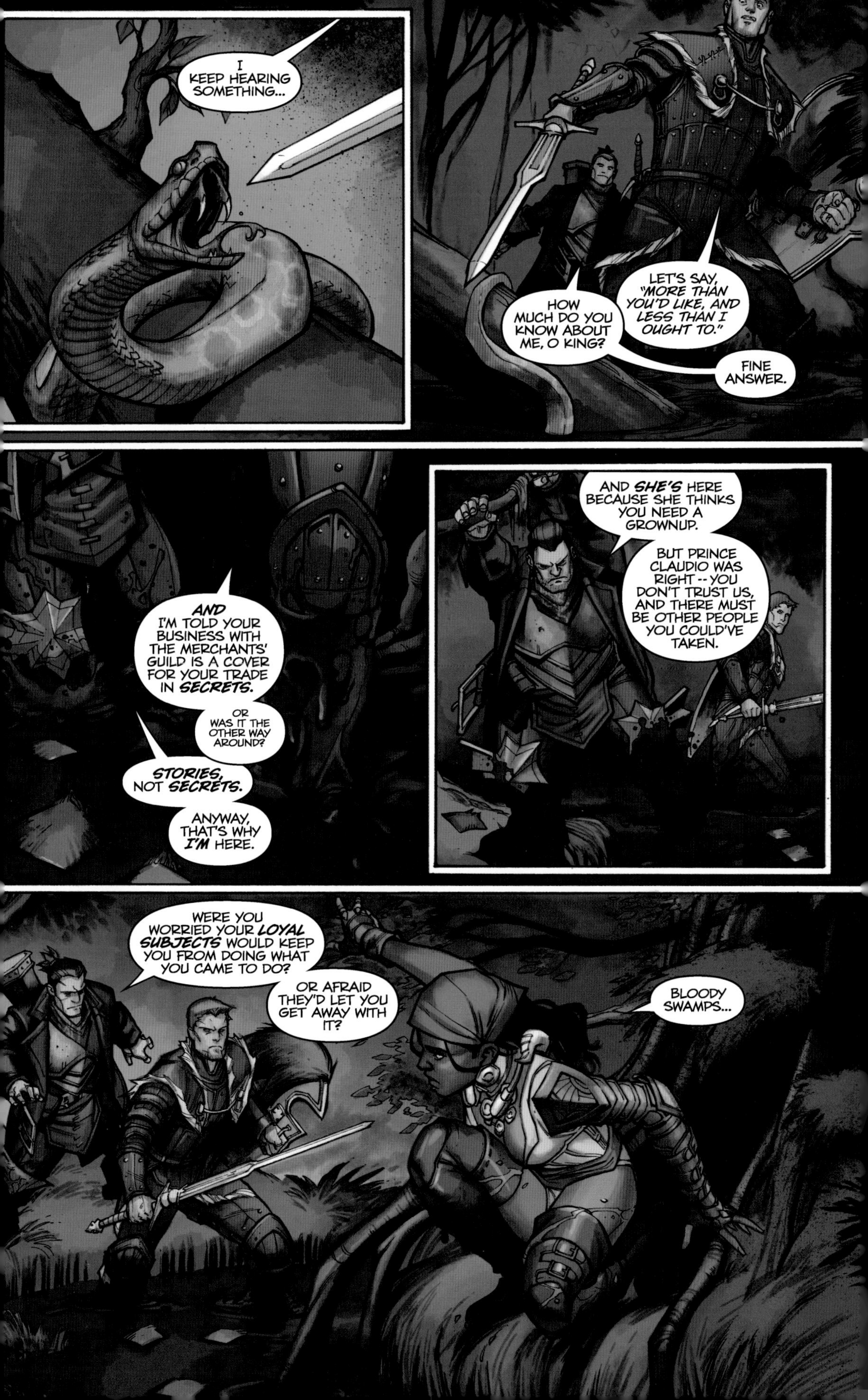

I KEEP HEARING SOMETHING...
HOW MUCH DO YOU KNOW ABOUT ME, O KING?
LET'S SAY, "MORE THAN YOU'D LIKE, AND LESS THAN I OUGHT TO."
FINE ANSWER.
AND I'M TOLD YOUR BUSINESS WITH THE MERCHANTS' GUILD IS A COVER FOR YOUR TRADE IN SECRETS.
OR WAS IT THE OTHER WAY AROUND?
STORIES, NOT SECRETS.
ANYWAY, THAT'S WHY I'M HERE.
AND SHE'S HERE BECAUSE SHE THINKS YOU NEED A GROWNUP.
BUT PRINCE CLAUDIO WAS RIGHT -- YOU DON'T TRUST US, AND THERE MUST BE OTHER PEOPLE YOU COULD'VE TAKEN.
WERE YOU WORRIED YOUR LOYAL SUBJECTS WOULD KEEP YOU FROM DOING WHAT YOU CAME TO DO?
OR AFRAID THEY'D LET YOU GET AWAY WITH IT?
BLOODY SWAMPS...

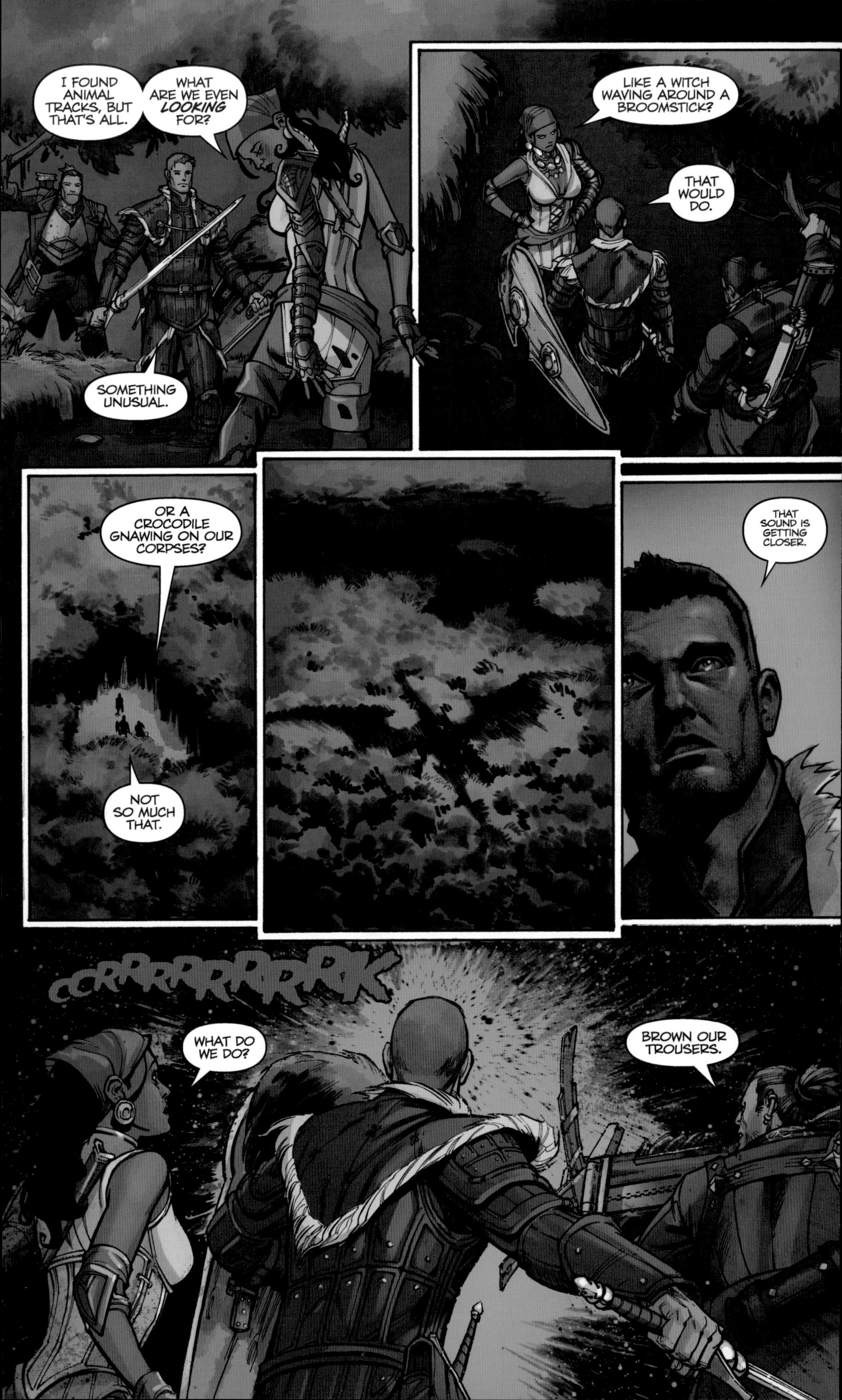
I FOUND ANIMAL TRACKS, BUT THAT'S ALL.
WHAT ARE WE EVEN *LOOKING* FOR?
SOMETHING UNUSUAL.
LIKE A WITCH WAVING AROUND A BROOMSTICK?
THAT WOULD DO.
OR A CROCODILE GNAWING ON OUR CORPSES?
NOT SO MUCH THAT.
THAT SOUND IS GETTING CLOSER.
CCRRRRRRRRRK
WHAT DO WE DO?
BROWN OUR TROUSERS.

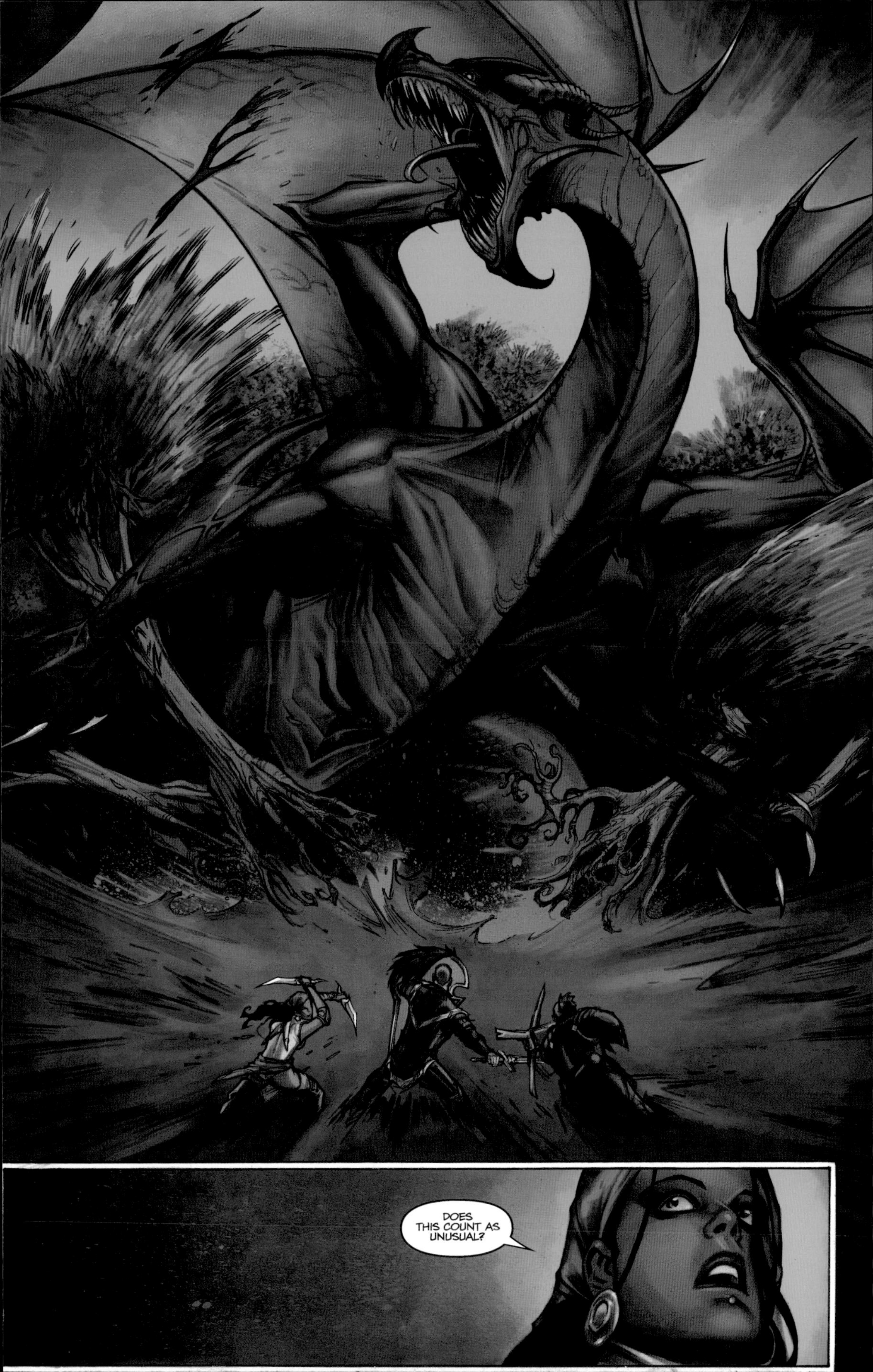
DOES THIS COUNT AS UNUSUAL?

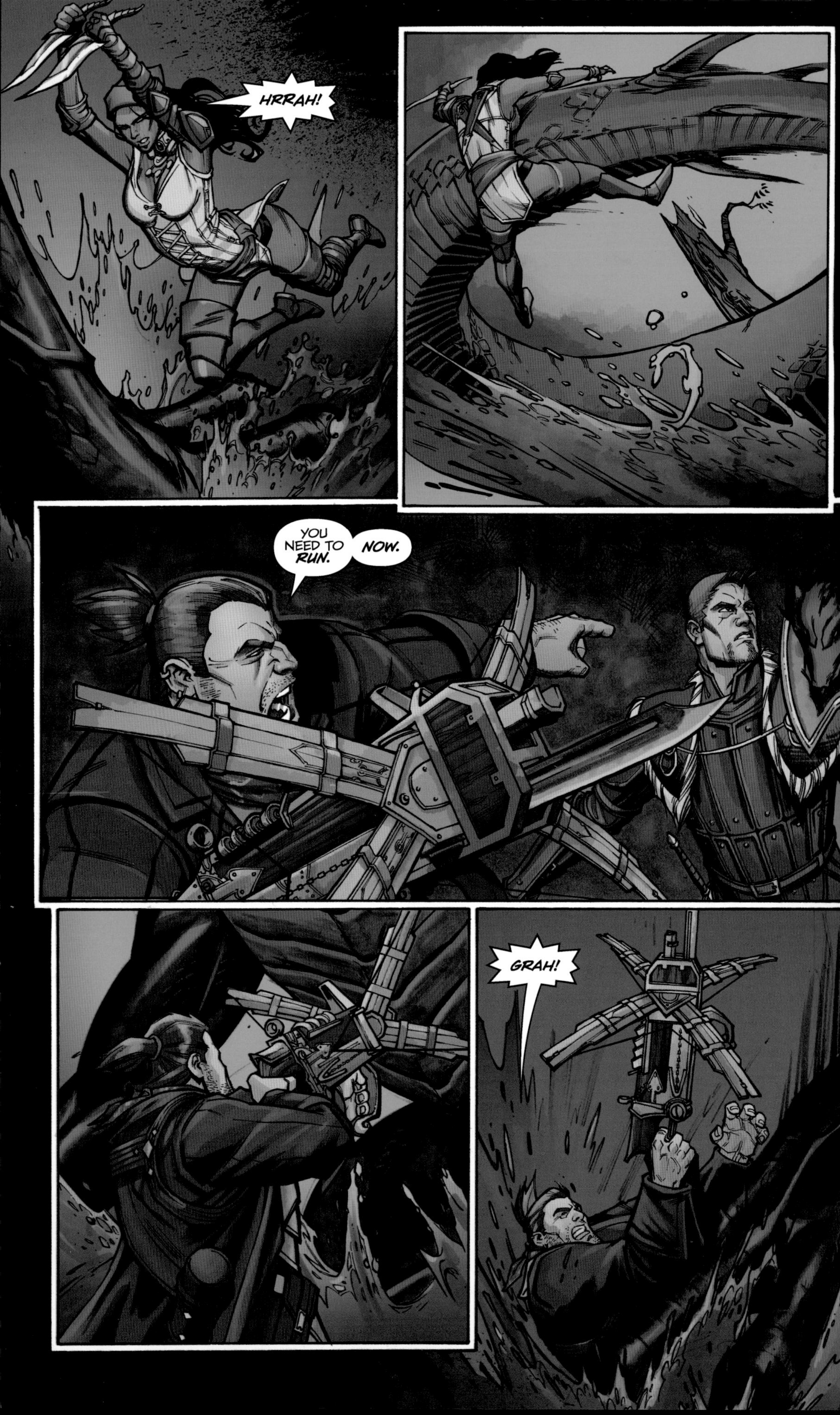
HRRAH!
YOU NEED TO RUN.
NOW.
GRAH!

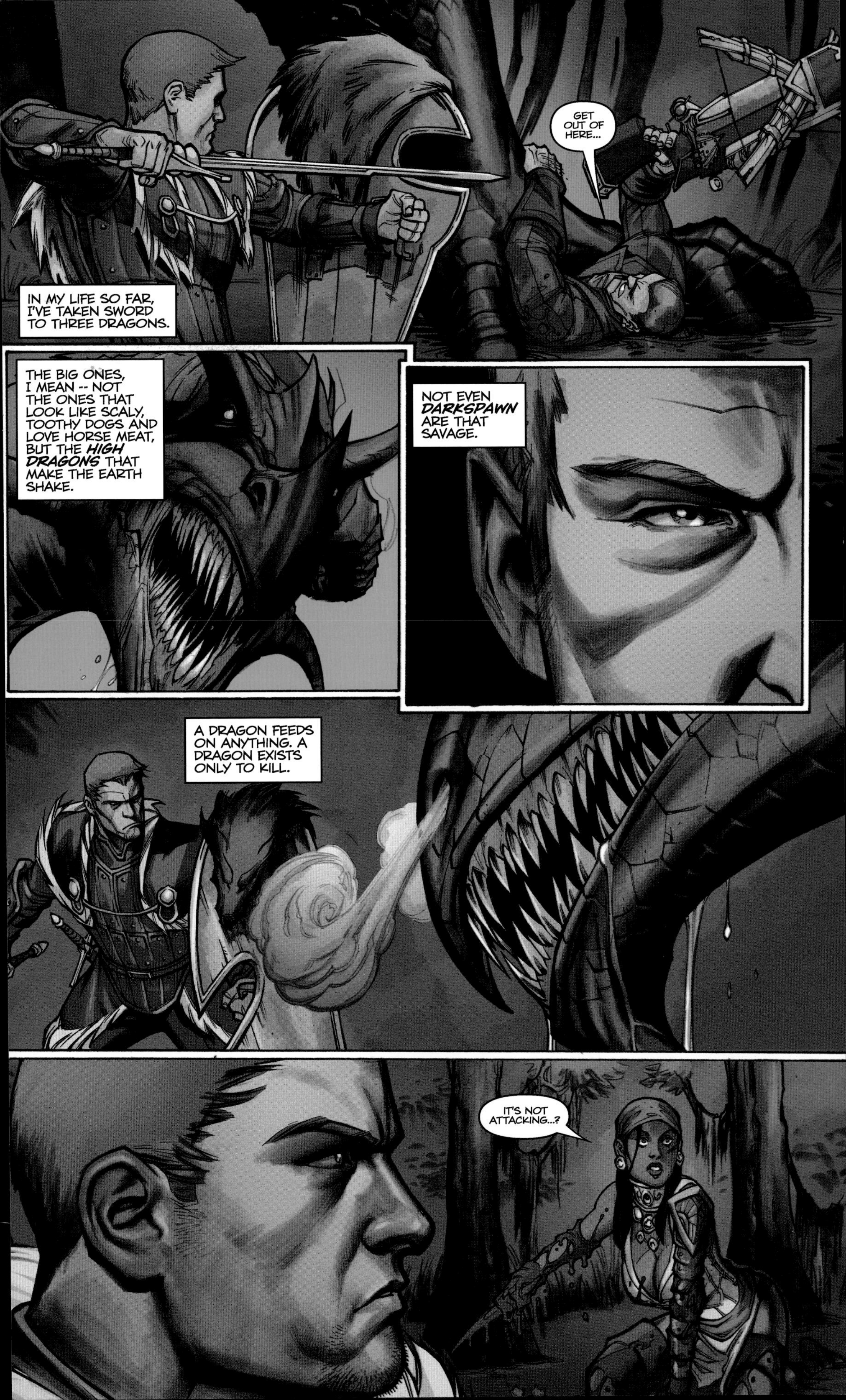
GET OUT OF HERE...
IN MY LIFE SO FAR, I'VE TAKEN SWORD TO THREE DRAGONS.
THE BIG ONES, I MEAN -- NOT THE ONES THAT LOOK LIKE SCALY, TOOTHY DOGS AND LOVE HORSE MEAT, BUT THE HIGH DRAGONS THAT MAKE THE EARTH SHAKE.
NOT EVEN DARKSPAWN ARE THAT SAVAGE.
A DRAGON FEEDS ON ANYTHING. A DRAGON EXISTS ONLY TO KILL.
IT'S NOT ATTACKING...?

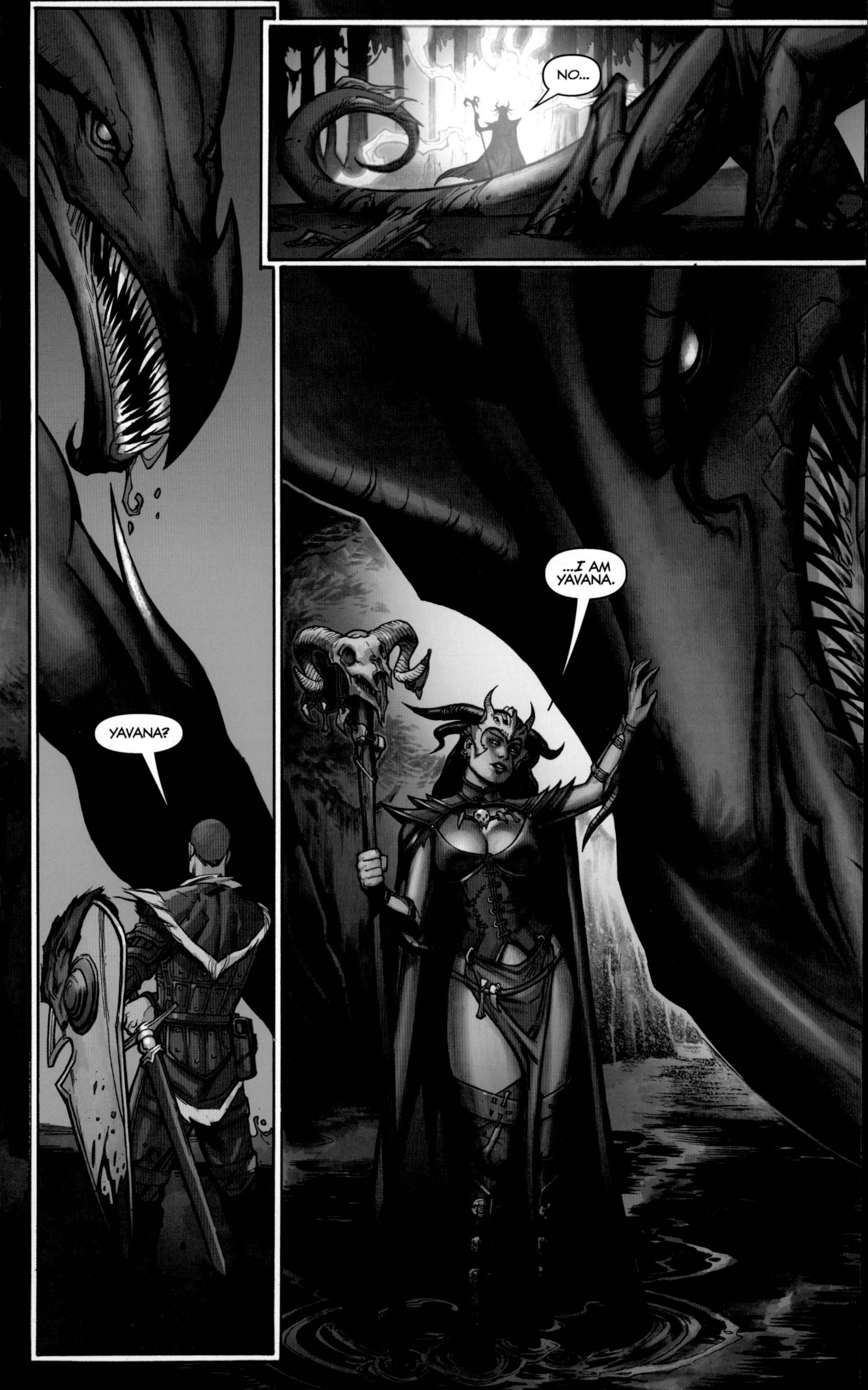
NO...
YAVANA?
...I AM YAVANA.

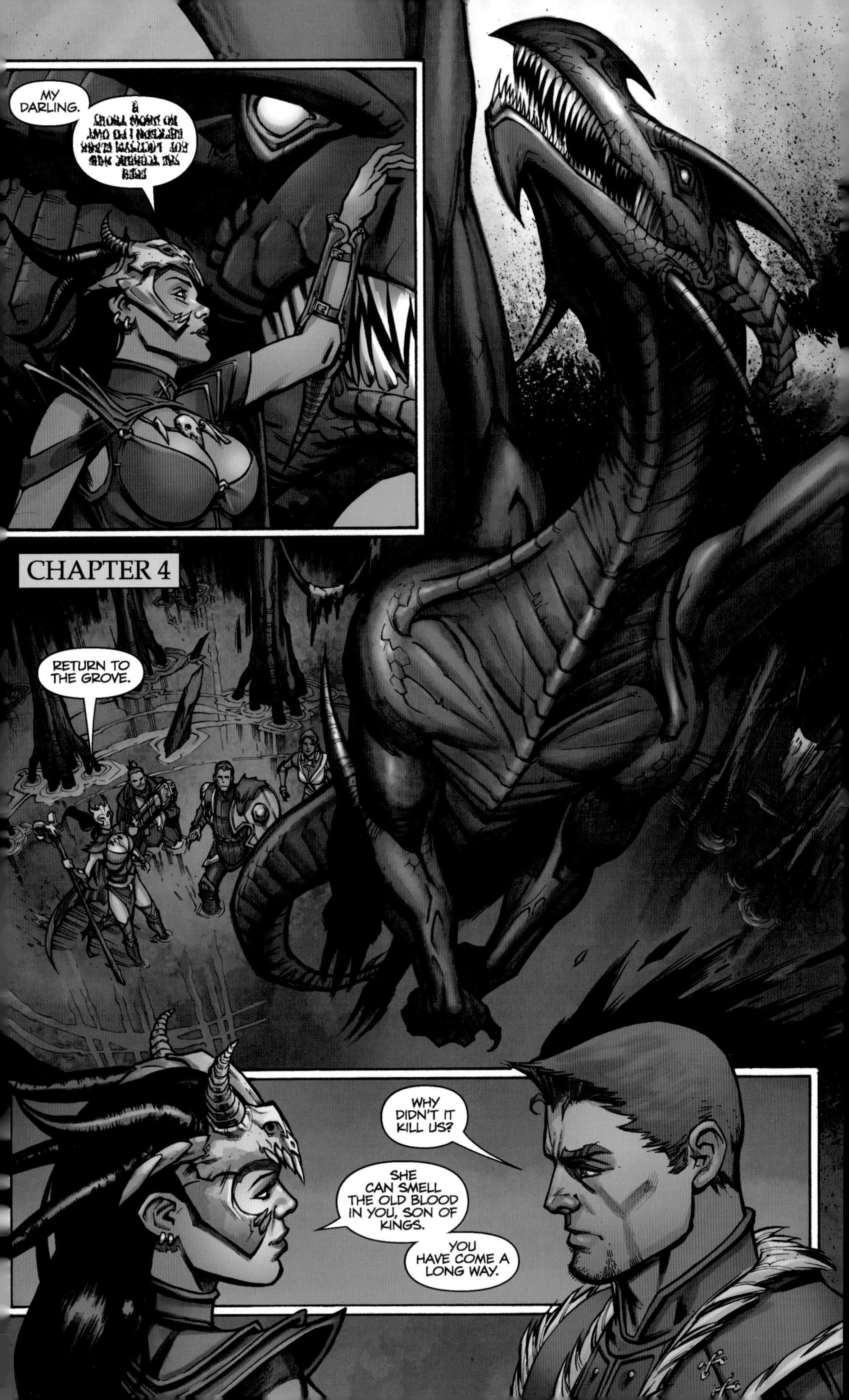
MY DARLING.
CHAPTER 4
RETURN TO THE GROVE.
WHY DIDN'T IT KILL US?
SHE CAN SMELL THE OLD BLOOD IN YOU, SON OF KINGS.
YOU HAVE COME A LONG WAY.

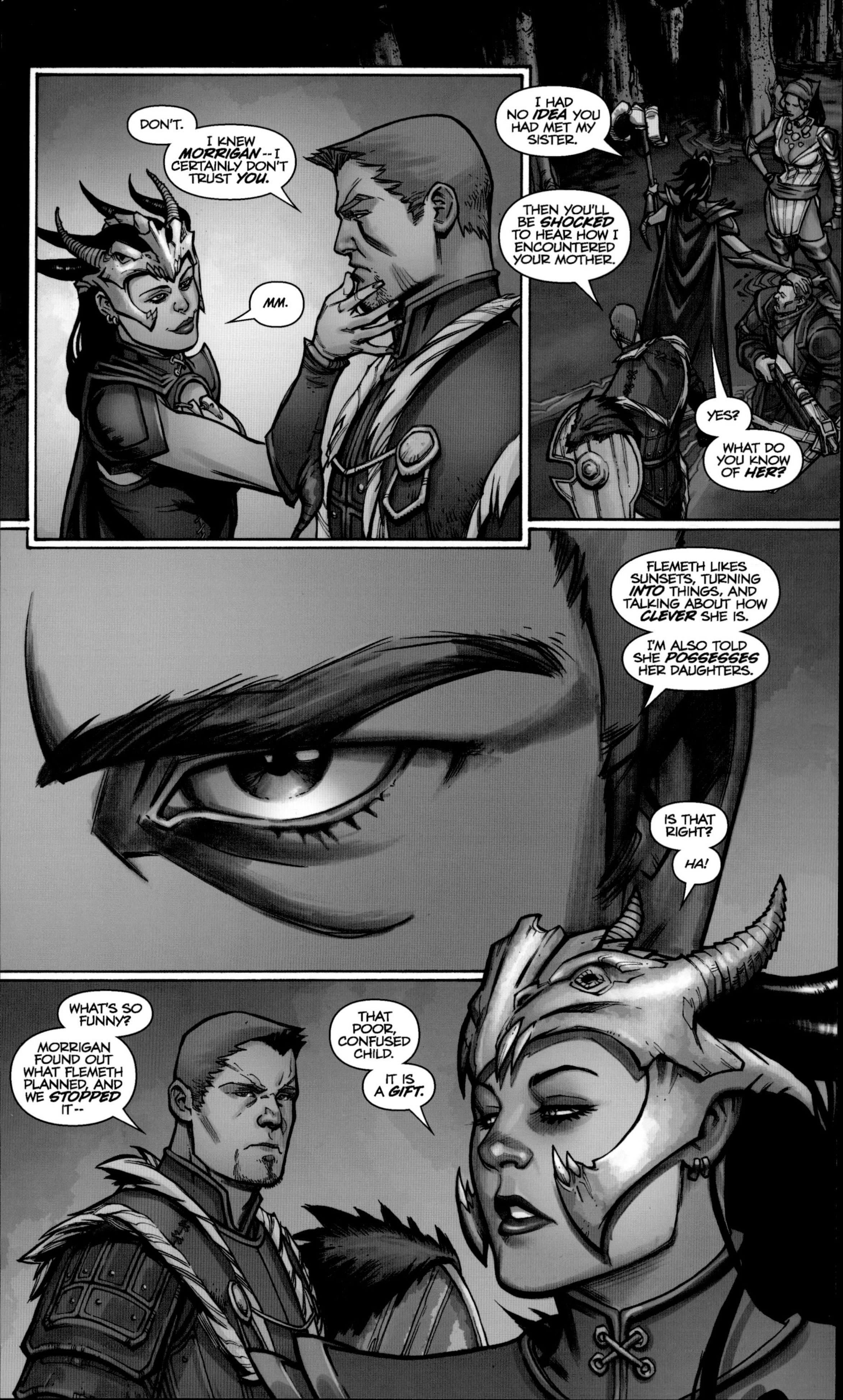
DON'T.
I KNEW MORRIGAN -- I CERTAINLY DON'T TRUST YOU.
MM.
I HAD NO IDEA YOU HAD MET MY SISTER.
THEN YOU'LL BE SHOCKED TO HEAR HOW I ENCOUNTERED YOUR MOTHER.
YES?
WHAT DO YOU KNOW OF HER?
FLEMETH LIKES SUNSETS, TURNING INTO THINGS, AND TALKING ABOUT HOW CLEVER SHE IS.
I'M ALSO TOLD SHE POSSESSES HER DAUGHTERS.
IS THAT RIGHT?
HA!
WHAT'S SO FUNNY?
MORRIGAN FOUND OUT WHAT FLEMETH PLANNED, AND WE STOPPED IT --
THAT POOR, CONFUSED CHILD.
IT IS A GIFT.

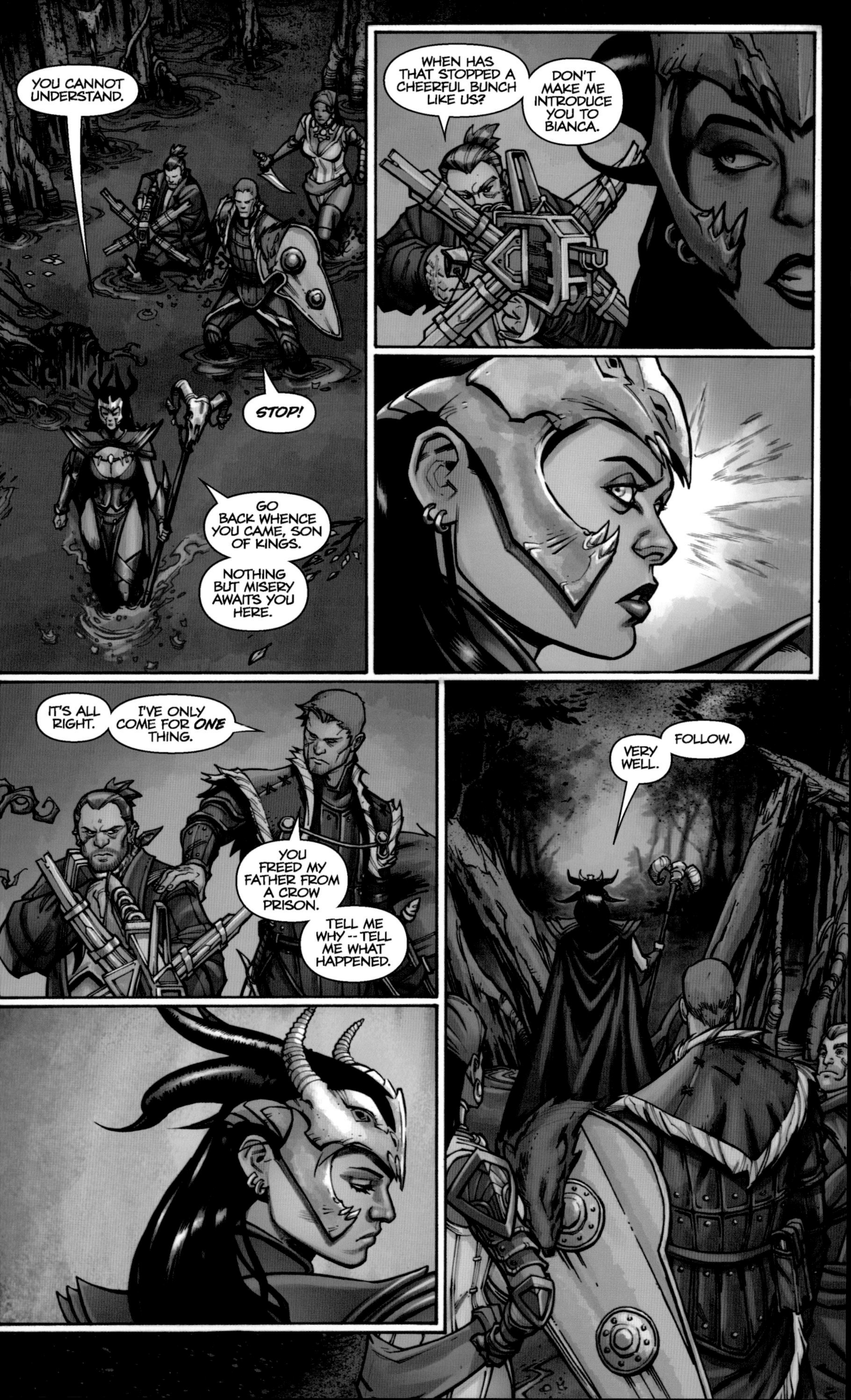
YOU CANNOT UNDERSTAND.
WHEN HAS THAT STOPPED A CHEERFUL BUNCH LIKE US?
DON'T MAKE ME INTRODUCE YOU TO BIANCA.
STOP!
GO BACK WHENCE YOU CAME, SON OF KINGS.
NOTHING BUT MISERY AWAITS YOU HERE.
IT'S ALL RIGHT.
I'VE ONLY COME FOR ONE THING.
YOU FREED MY FATHER FROM A CROW PRISON.
TELL ME WHY -- TELL ME WHAT HAPPENED.
VERY WELL.
FOLLOW.

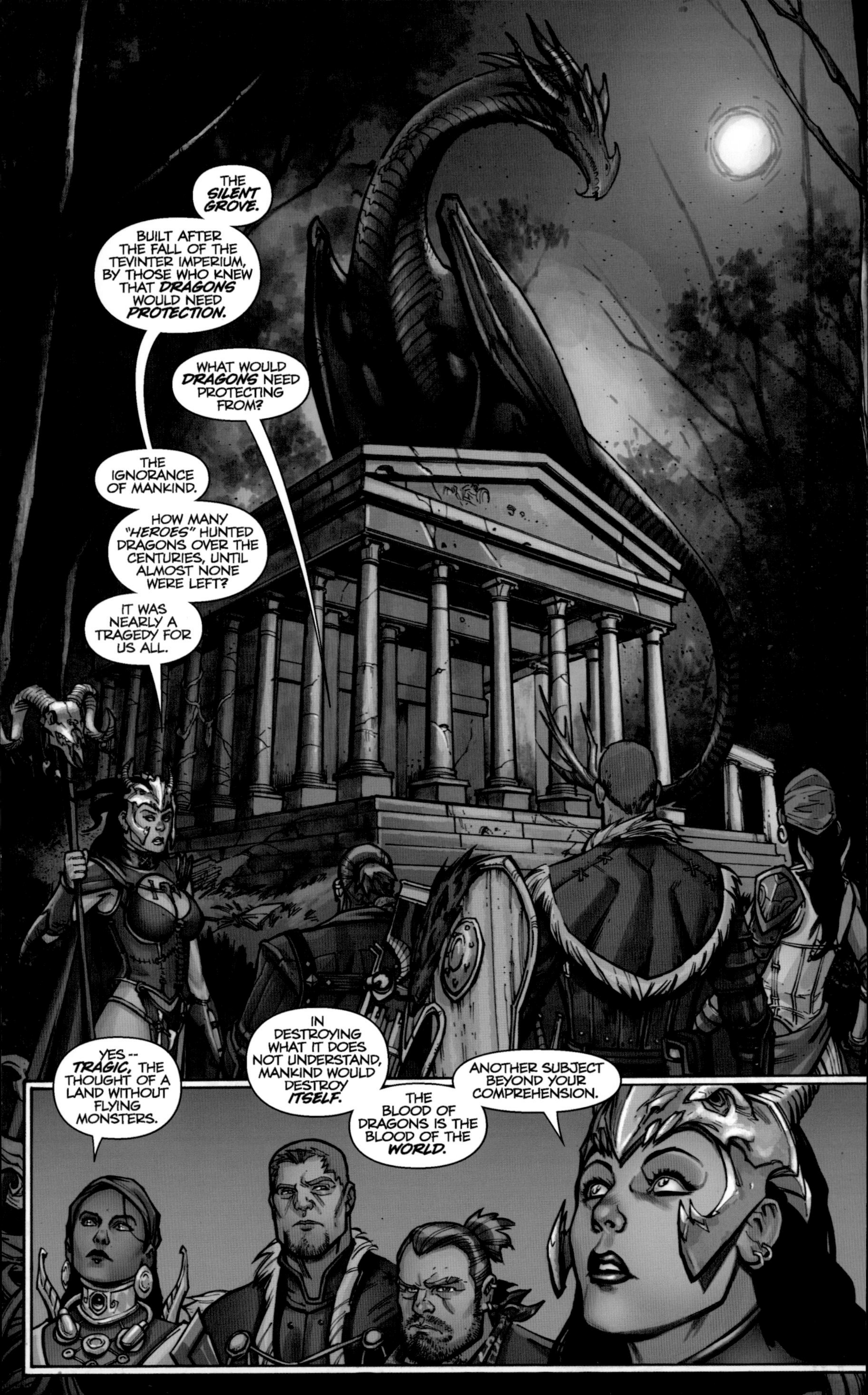

THE SILENT GROVE.
BUILT AFTER THE FALL OF THE TEVINTER IMPERIUM, BY THOSE WHO KNEW THAT DRAGONS WOULD NEED PROTECTION.
WHAT WOULD DRAGONS NEED PROTECTING FROM?
THE IGNORANCE OF MANKIND.
HOW MANY "HEROES" HUNTED DRAGONS OVER THE CENTURIES, UNTIL ALMOST NONE WERE LEFT?
IT WAS NEARLY A TRAGEDY FOR US ALL.
YES -- TRAGIC, THE THOUGHT OF A LAND WITHOUT FLYING MONSTERS.
IN DESTROYING WHAT IT DOES NOT UNDERSTAND, MANKIND WOULD DESTROY ITSELF.
THE BLOOD OF DRAGONS IS THE BLOOD OF THE WORLD.
ANOTHER SUBJECT BEYOND YOUR COMPREHENSION.

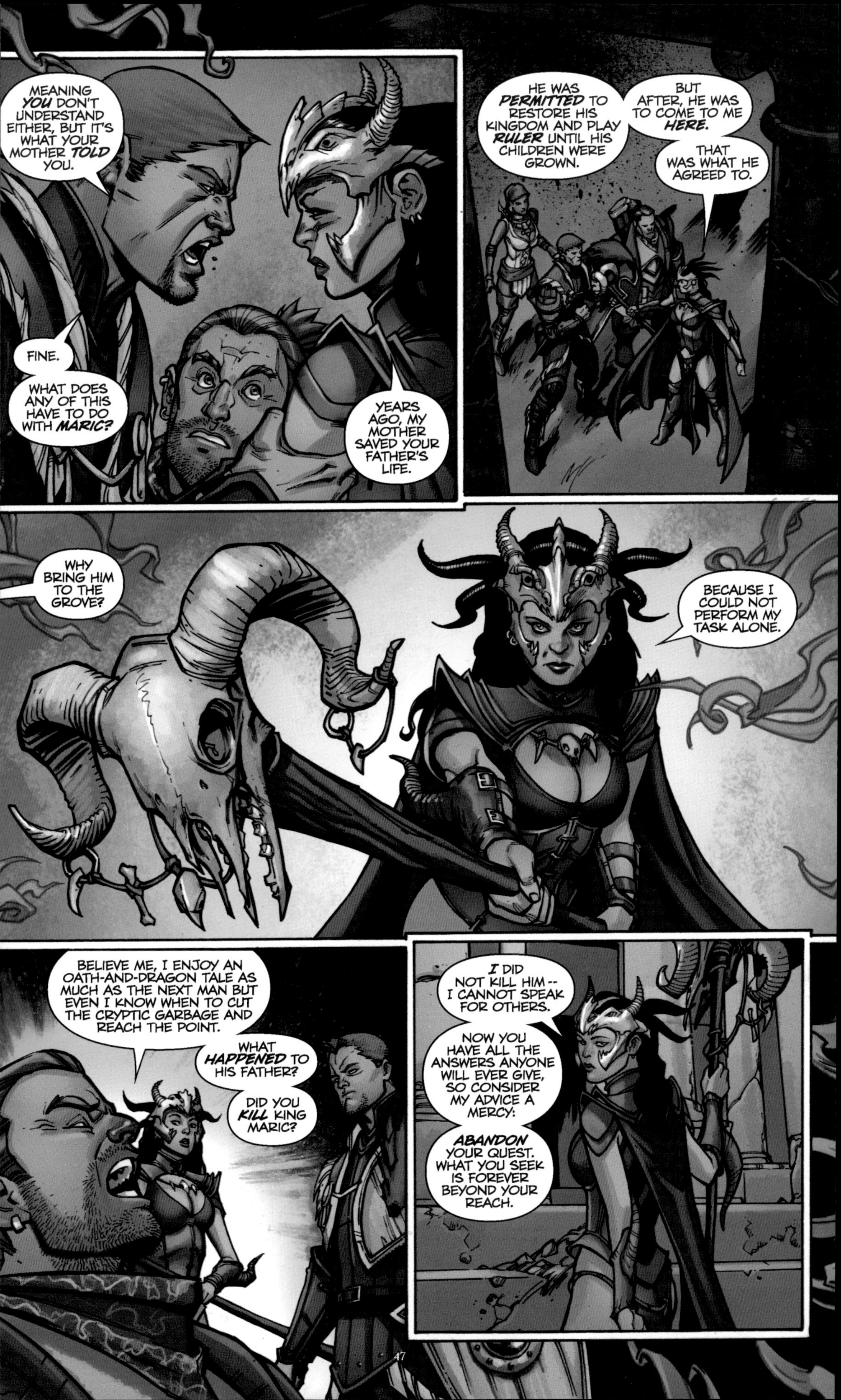
MEANING YOU DON'T UNDERSTAND EITHER, BUT IT'S WHAT YOUR MOTHER TOLD YOU.
FINE.
WHAT DOES ANY OF THIS HAVE TO DO WITH MARIC?
YEARS AGO, MY MOTHER SAVED YOUR FATHER'S LIFE.
HE WAS PERMITTED TO RESTORE HIS KINGDOM AND PLAY RULER UNTIL HIS CHILDREN WERE GROWN.
BUT AFTER, HE WAS TO COME TO ME HERE.
THAT WAS WHAT HE AGREED TO.
WHY BRING HIM TO THE GROVE?
BECAUSE I COULD NOT PERFORM MY TASK ALONE.
BELIEVE ME, I ENJOY AN OATH-AND-DRAGON TALE AS MUCH AS THE NEXT MAN BUT EVEN I KNOW WHEN TO CUT THE CRYPTIC GARBAGE AND REACH THE POINT.
WHAT HAPPENED TO HIS FATHER?
DID YOU KILL KING MARIC?
I DID NOT KILL HIM -- I CANNOT SPEAK FOR OTHERS.
NOW YOU HAVE ALL THE ANSWERS ANYONE WILL EVER GIVE, SO CONSIDER MY ADVICE A MERCY:
ABANDON YOUR QUEST. WHAT YOU SEEK IS FOREVER BEYOND YOUR REACH.

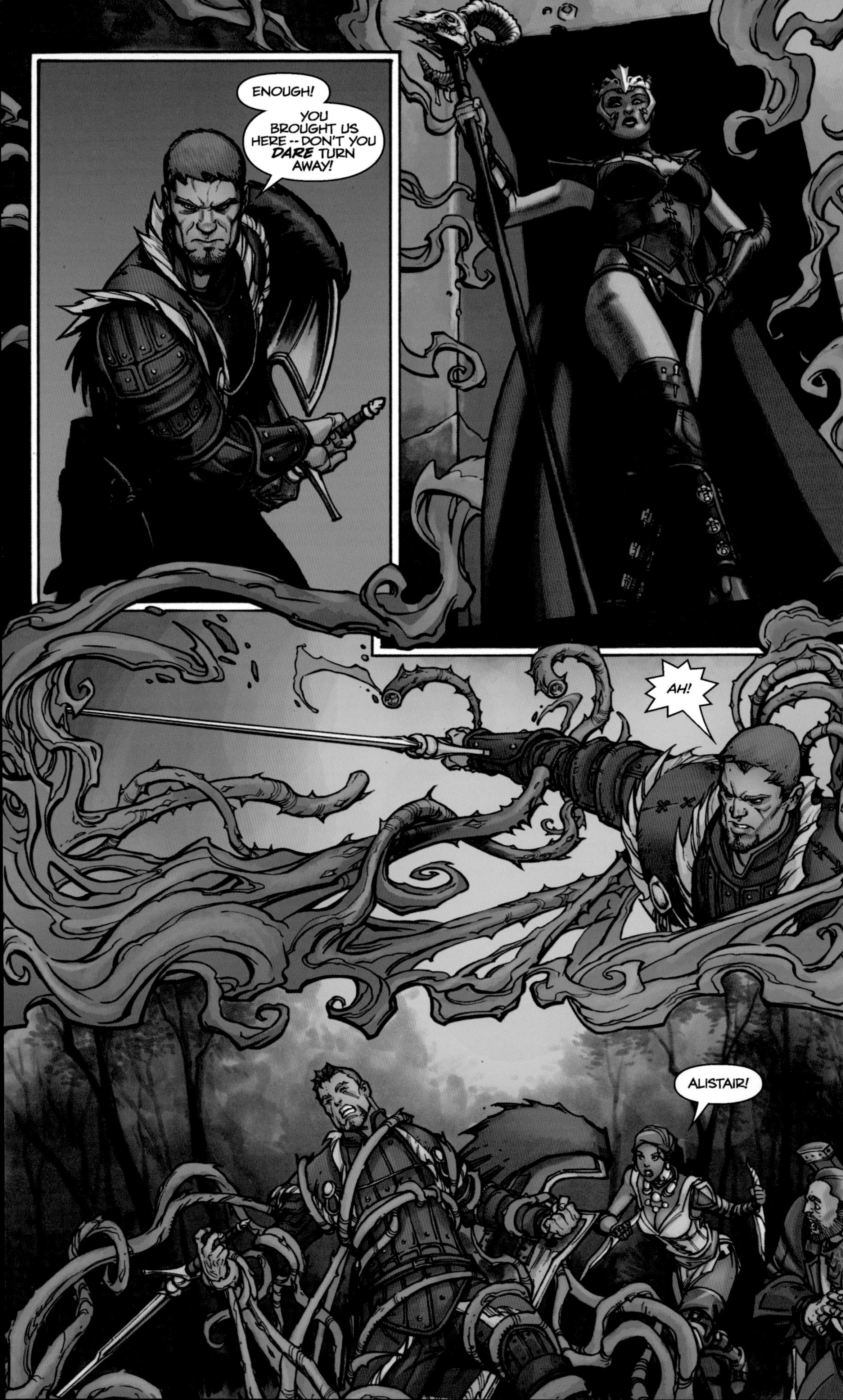
ENOUGH!
YOU BROUGHT US HERE -- DON'T YOU DARE TURN AWAY!
AH!
ALISTAIR!

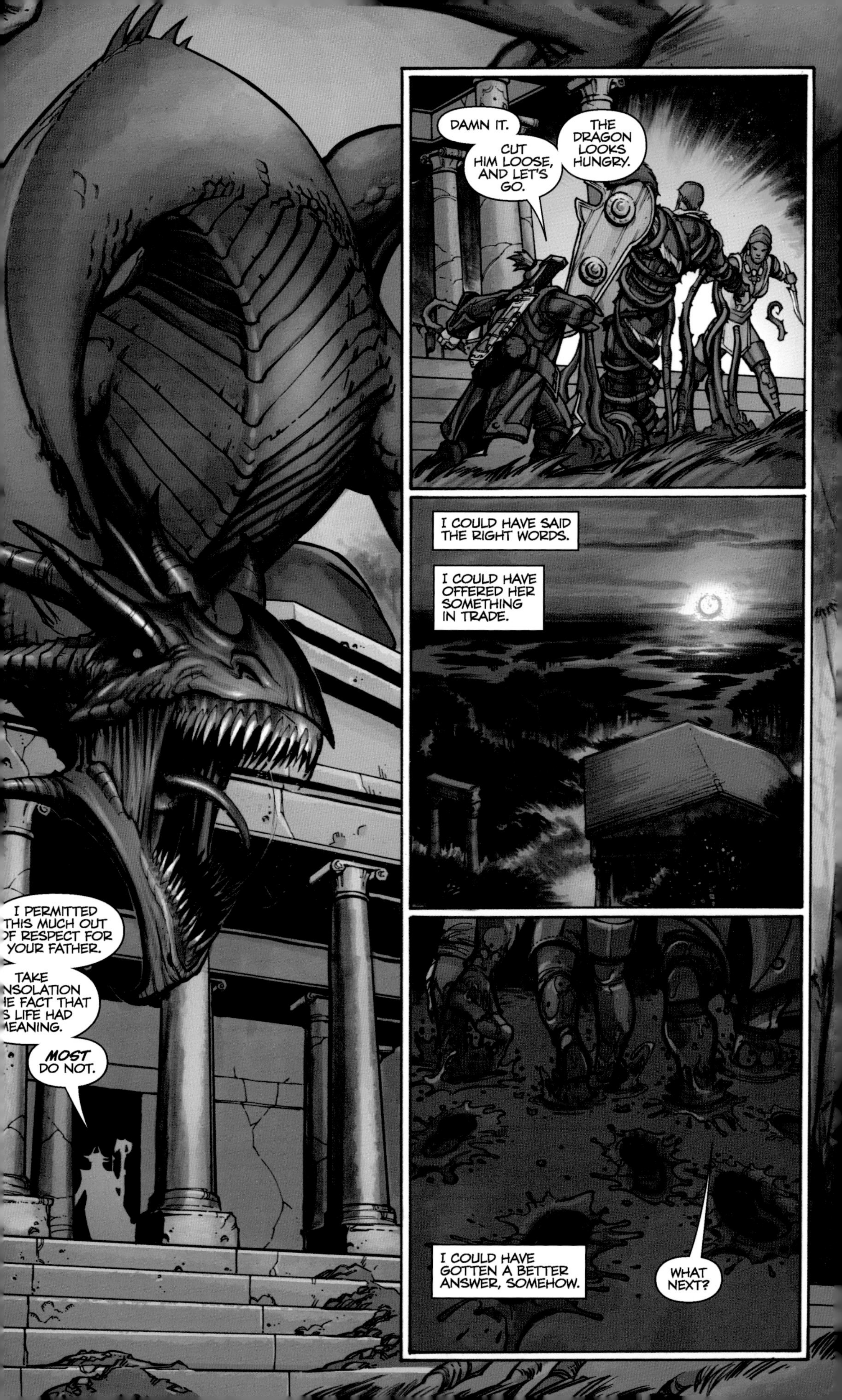

I PERMITTED THIS MUCH OUT)F RESPECT FOR YOUR FATHER.
TAKE NSOLATION HE FACT THAT S LIFE HAD EANING.
MOST DO NOT.
DAMN IT.
CUT HIM LOOSE, AND LET'S GO.
THE DRAGON LOOKS HUNGRY.
I COULD HAVE SAID THE RIGHT WORDS.
I COULD HAVE OFFERED HER SOMETHING IN TRADE.
I COULD HAVE GOTTEN A BETTER ANSWER, SOMEHOW.
WHAT NEXT?

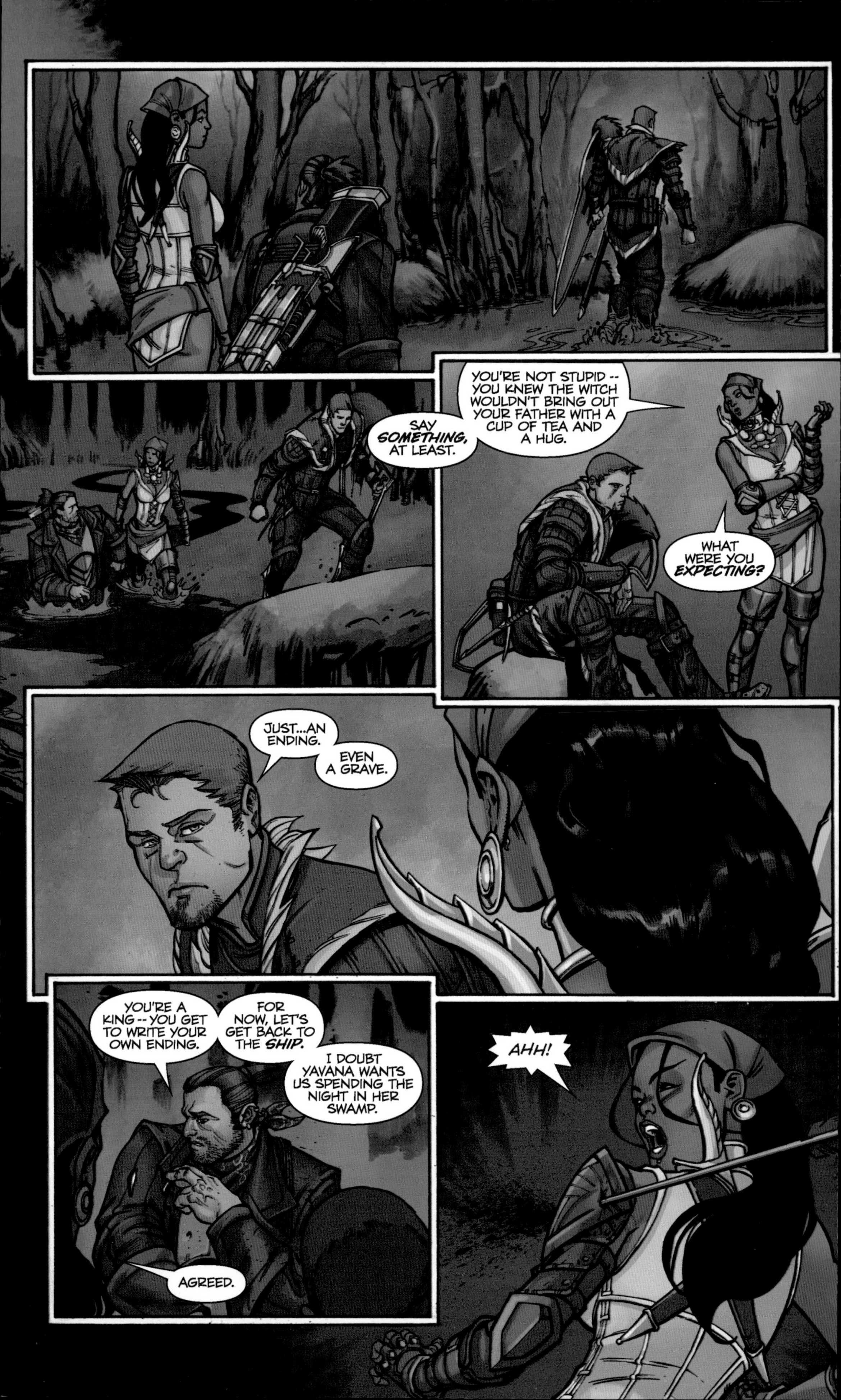

SAY SOMETHING, AT LEAST.
YOU'RE NOT STUPID -- YOU KNEW THE WITCH WOULDN'T BRING OUT YOUR FATHER WITH A CUP OF TEA AND A HUG.
WHAT WERE YOU EXPECTING?
JUST...AN ENDING.
EVEN A GRAVE.
YOU'RE A KING -- YOU GET TO WRITE YOUR OWN ENDING.
FOR NOW, LET'S GET BACK TO THE SHIP.
I DOUBT YAVANA WANTS US SPENDING THE NIGHT IN HER SWAMP.
AGREED.
AHH!

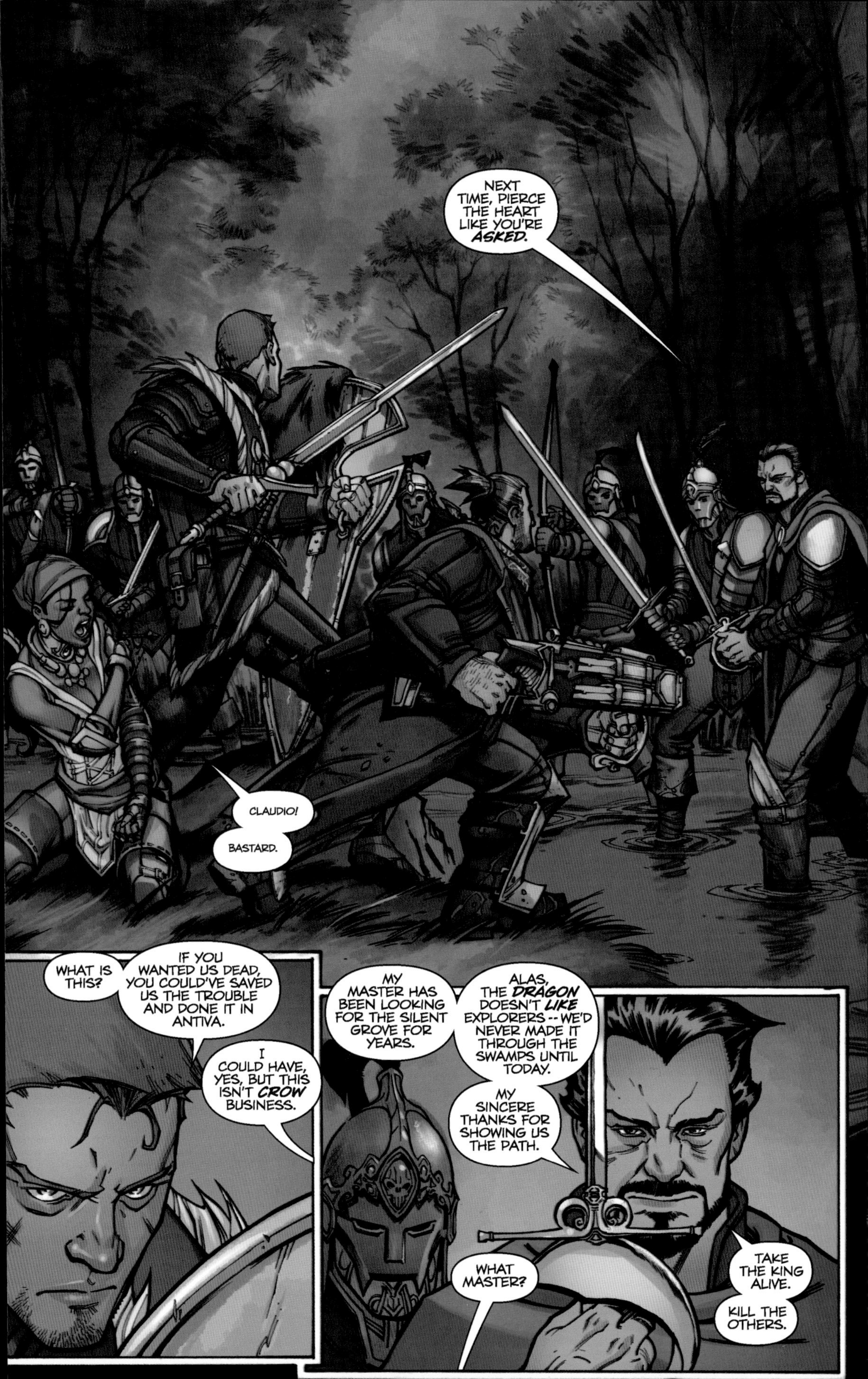
NEXT TIME, PIERCE THE HEART LIKE YOU'RE ASKED.
CLAUDIO!
BASTARD.
WHAT IS THIS?
IF YOU WANTED US DEAD, YOU COULD'VE SAVED US THE TROUBLE AND DONE IT IN ANTIVA.
I COULD HAVE, YES, BUT THIS ISN'T CROW BUSINESS.
MY MASTER HAS BEEN LOOKING FOR THE SILENT GROVE FOR YEARS.
ALAS, THE DRAGON DOESN'T LIKE EXPLORERS -- WE'D NEVER MADE IT THROUGH THE SWAMPS UNTIL TODAY.
MY SINCERE THANKS FOR SHOWING US THE PATH.
WHAT MASTER?
TAKE THE KING ALIVE.
KILL THE OTHERS.

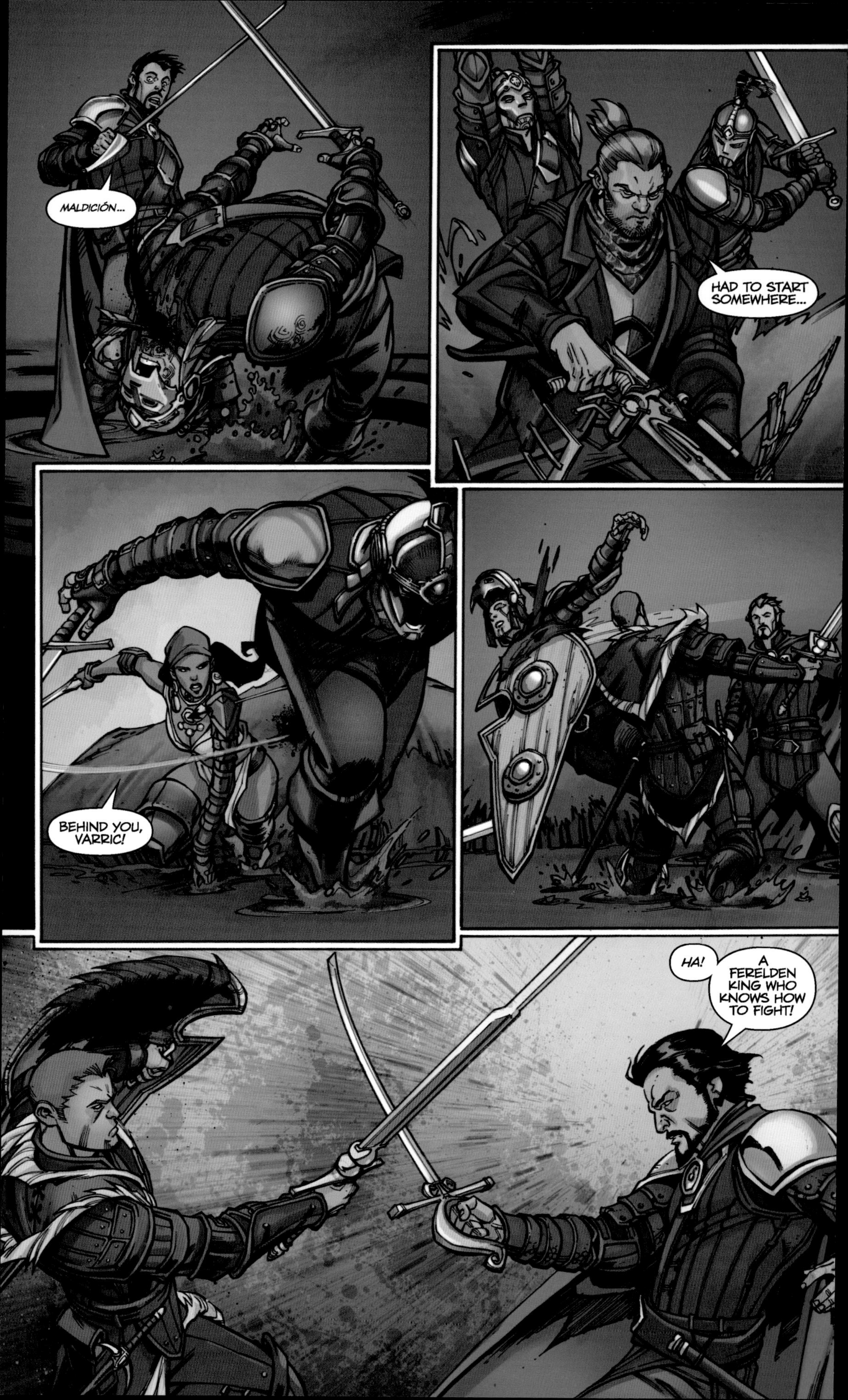
MALDICIÓN...
HAD TO START SOMEWHERE...
BEHIND YOU, VARRIC!
HA!
A FERELDEN KING WHO KNOWS HOW TO FIGHT!

STOP! WE SURRENDER.

WHAT?

IF YOU WANT ME ALIVE, YOU LET ISABELA AND VARRIC GO.

THEN I SURRENDER.

DON'T EVEN THINK OF IT.

CLAUDIO'S A *WORM* AND WE'RE ALL STILL BREATHING.

I HAVEN'T HAD THIS MUCH FUN SINCE -- AH!

SINCE YOU WERE BEING CHASED BY QUNARI?

I WAS THINKING... ANSELMO'S BACHELOR PARTY.

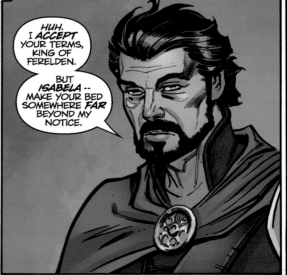

HUH. I *ACCEPT* YOUR TERMS, KING OF FERELDEN.

BUT *ISABELA* -- MAKE YOUR BED SOMEWHERE *FAR* BEYOND MY NOTICE.

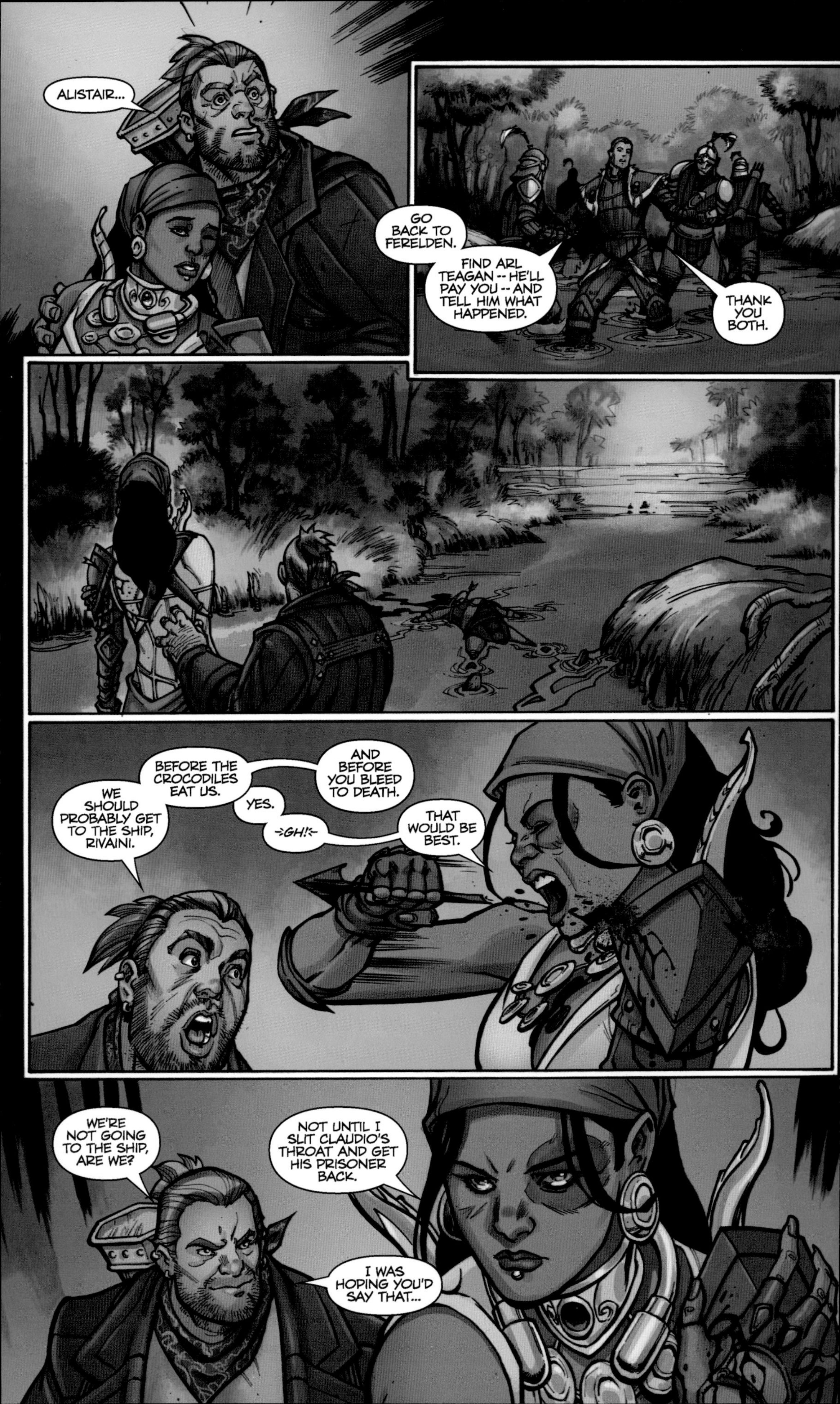
ALISTAIR...
GO BACK TO FERELDEN.
FIND ARL TEAGAN -- HE'LL PAY YOU -- AND TELL HIM WHAT HAPPENED.
THANK YOU BOTH.
WE SHOULD PROBABLY GET TO THE SHIP, RIVAINI.
BEFORE THE CROCODILES EAT US.
AND BEFORE YOU BLEED TO DEATH.
YES.
-GH!-
THAT WOULD BE BEST.
WE'RE NOT GOING TO THE SHIP, ARE WE?
NOT UNTIL I SLIT CLAUDIO'S THROAT AND GET HIS PRISONER BACK.
I WAS HOPING YOU'D SAY THAT...

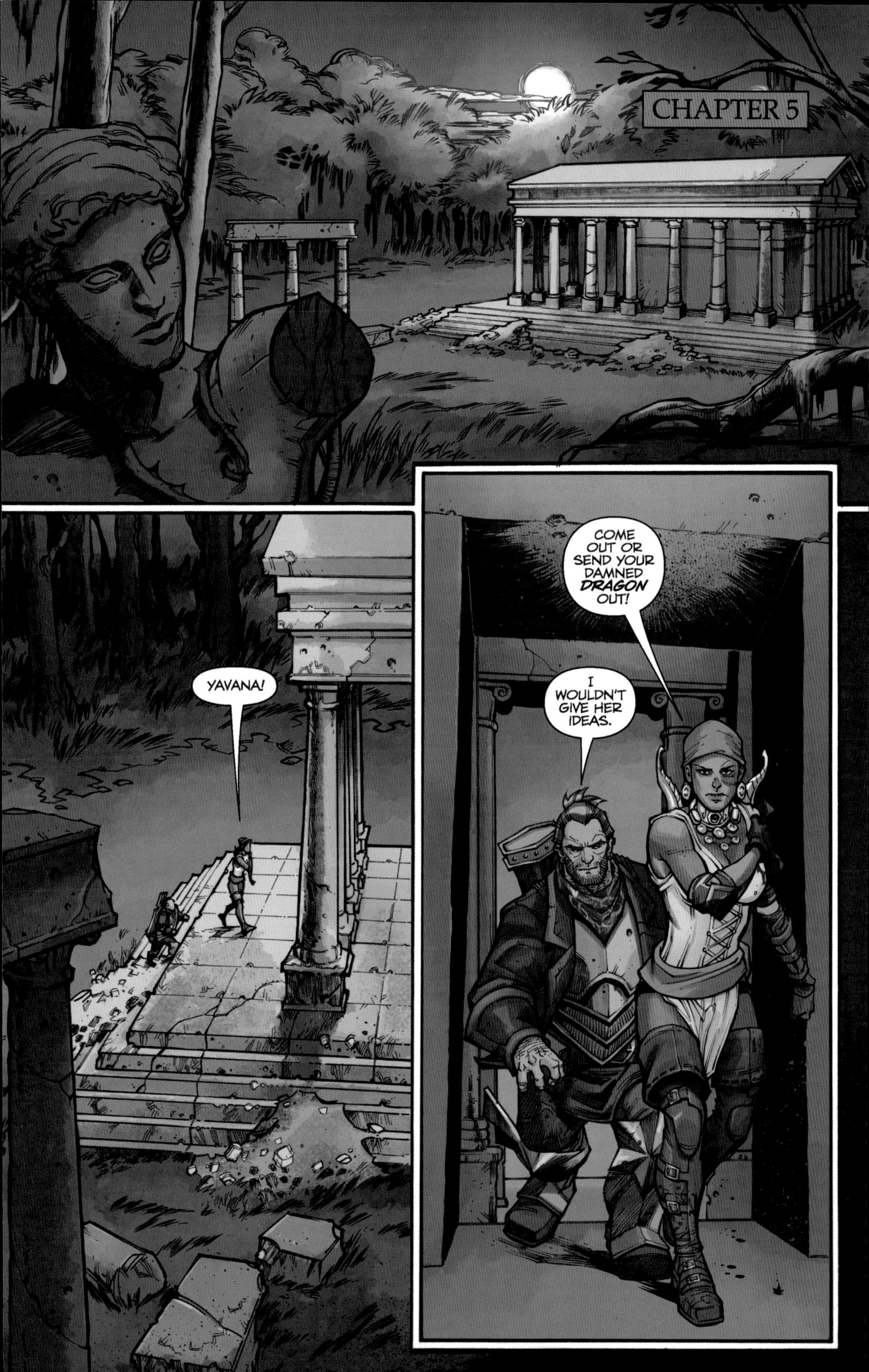
CHAPTER 5
YAVANA!
COME OUT OR SEND YOUR DAMNED DRAGON OUT!
I WOULDN'T GIVE HER IDEAS.

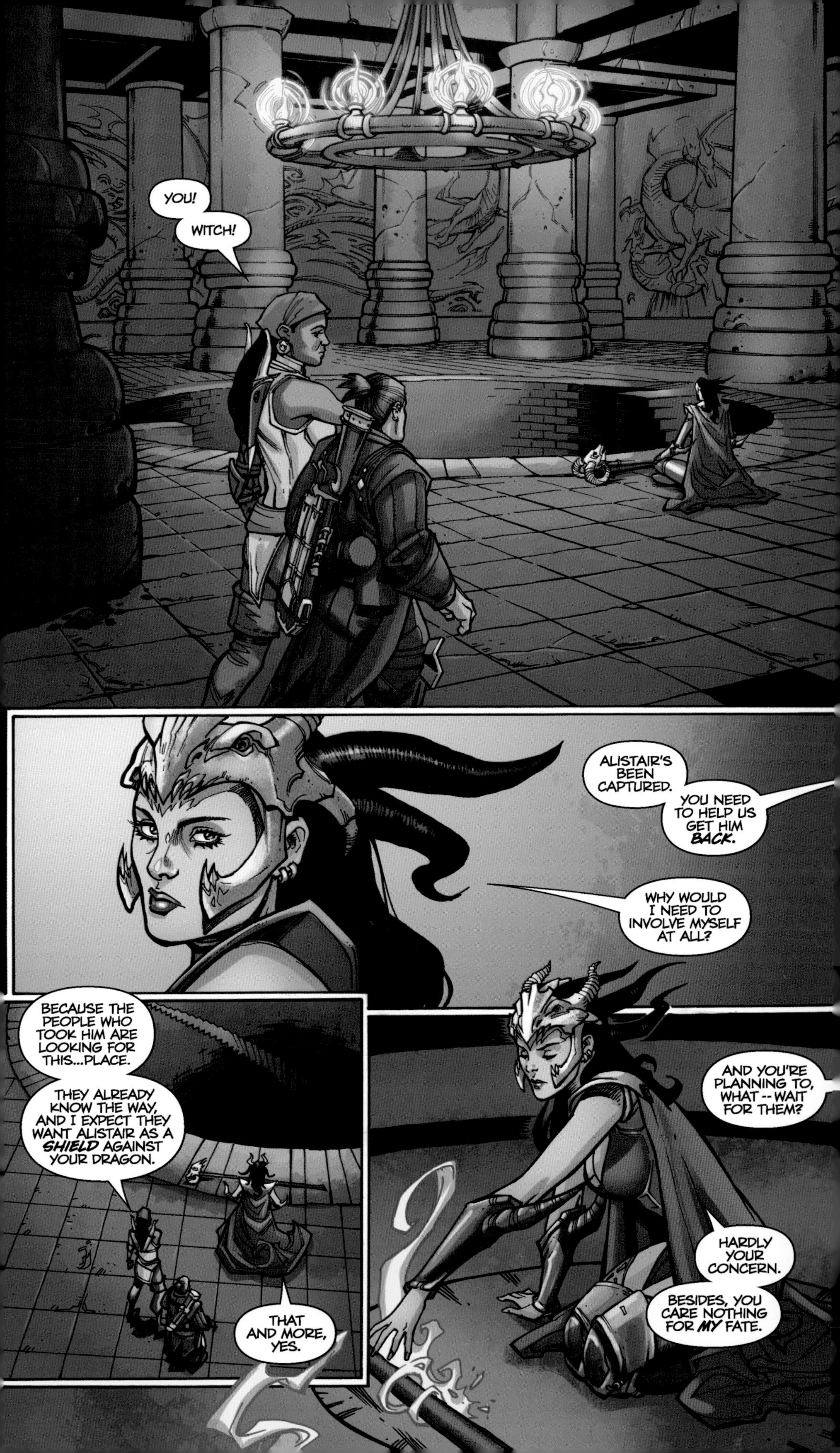
YOU!
WITCH!
ALISTAIR'S BEEN CAPTURED.
YOU NEED TO HELP US GET HIM *BACK*.
WHY WOULD I NEED TO INVOLVE MYSELF AT ALL?
BECAUSE THE PEOPLE WHO TOOK HIM ARE LOOKING FOR THIS...PLACE.
THEY ALREADY KNOW THE WAY, AND I EXPECT THEY WANT ALISTAIR AS A *SHIELD* AGAINST YOUR DRAGON.
THAT AND MORE, YES.
AND YOU'RE PLANNING TO, WHAT -- WAIT FOR THEM?
HARDLY YOUR CONCERN.
BESIDES, YOU CARE NOTHING FOR *MY* FATE.

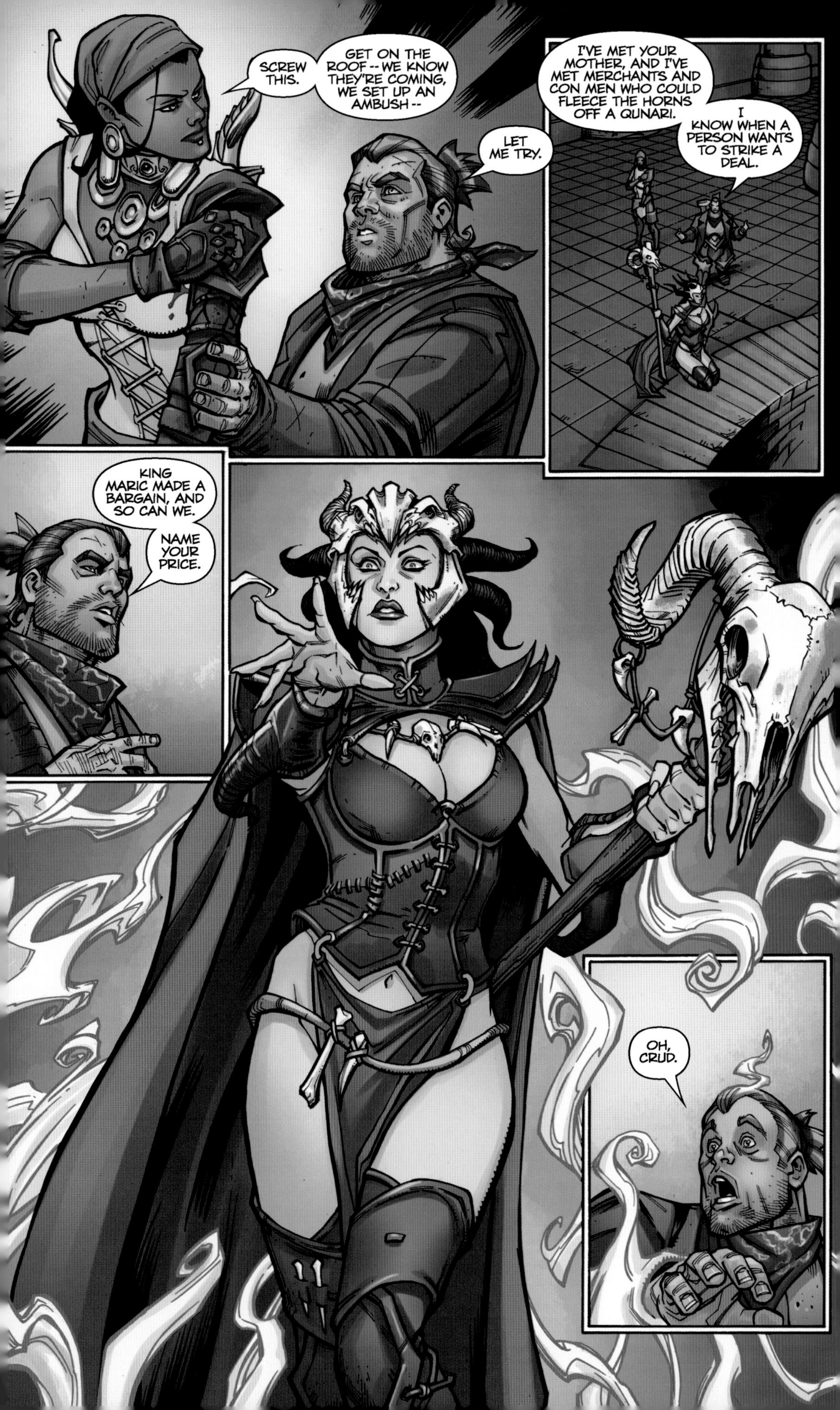
SCREW THIS.
GET ON THE ROOF -- WE KNOW THEY'RE COMING, WE SET UP AN AMBUSH --
LET ME TRY.
I'VE MET YOUR MOTHER, AND I'VE MET MERCHANTS AND CON MEN WHO COULD FLEECE THE HORNS OFF A QUNARI.
I KNOW WHEN A PERSON WANTS TO STRIKE A DEAL.
KING MARIC MADE A BARGAIN, AND SO CAN WE.
NAME YOUR PRICE.
OH, CRUD.

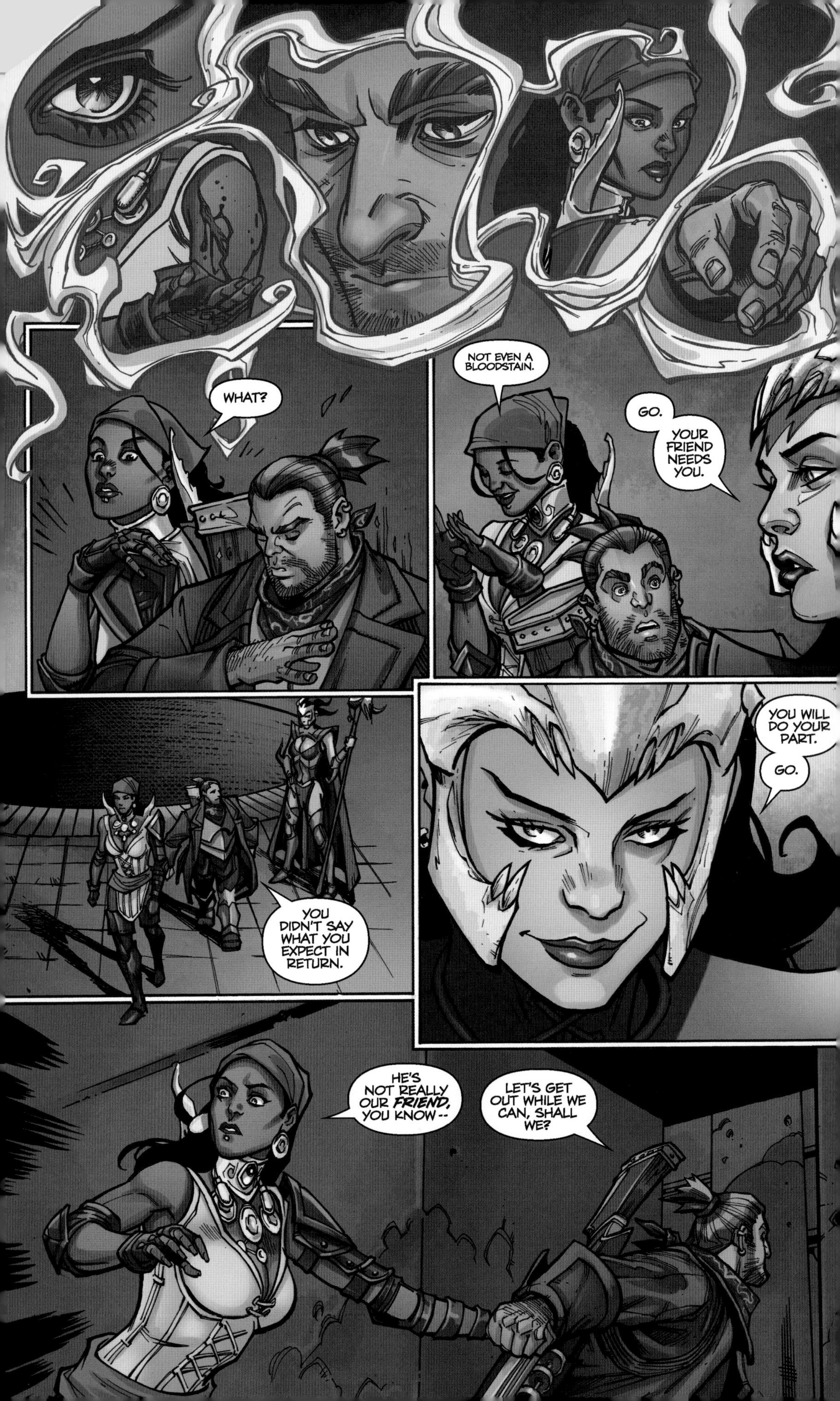
WHAT?
NOT EVEN A BLOODSTAIN.
GO.
YOUR FRIEND NEEDS YOU.
YOU DIDN'T SAY WHAT YOU EXPECT IN RETURN.
YOU WILL DO YOUR PART.
GO.
HE'S NOT REALLY OUR *FRIEND,* YOU KNOW--
LET'S GET OUT WHILE WE CAN, SHALL WE?

...IF IT'S ANY COMFORT, I WAS *IMPRESSED* YOU CAME TO ANTIVA ALONE.

IT SHOWED *COURAGE,* IF NOT *INTELLECT.*

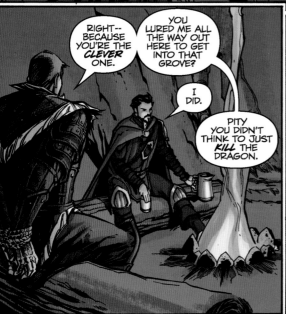

RIGHT-- BECAUSE YOU'RE THE *CLEVER* ONE.

YOU LURED ME ALL THE WAY OUT HERE TO GET INTO THAT GROVE?

I DID.

PITY YOU DIDN'T THINK TO JUST *KILL* THE DRAGON.

WE TOYED WITH THE NOTION OF *TRYING* --

-- BUT THAT BEAUTY IS WHY WE'RE INTERESTED.

WHEN YOU SAY *"WE"*...YOU'RE NOT TALKING ABOUT THE CROW ASSASSINS.

WE ALL HAVE OUR PATRONS.

PROVE MORE TOLERABLE THAN YOUR *FATHER,* AND I MAY EVEN TELL YOU ABOUT MINE.

WHAT DO YOU KNOW ABOUT MARIC?

WHAT *HAPPENED* AFTER HE CAME HERE?

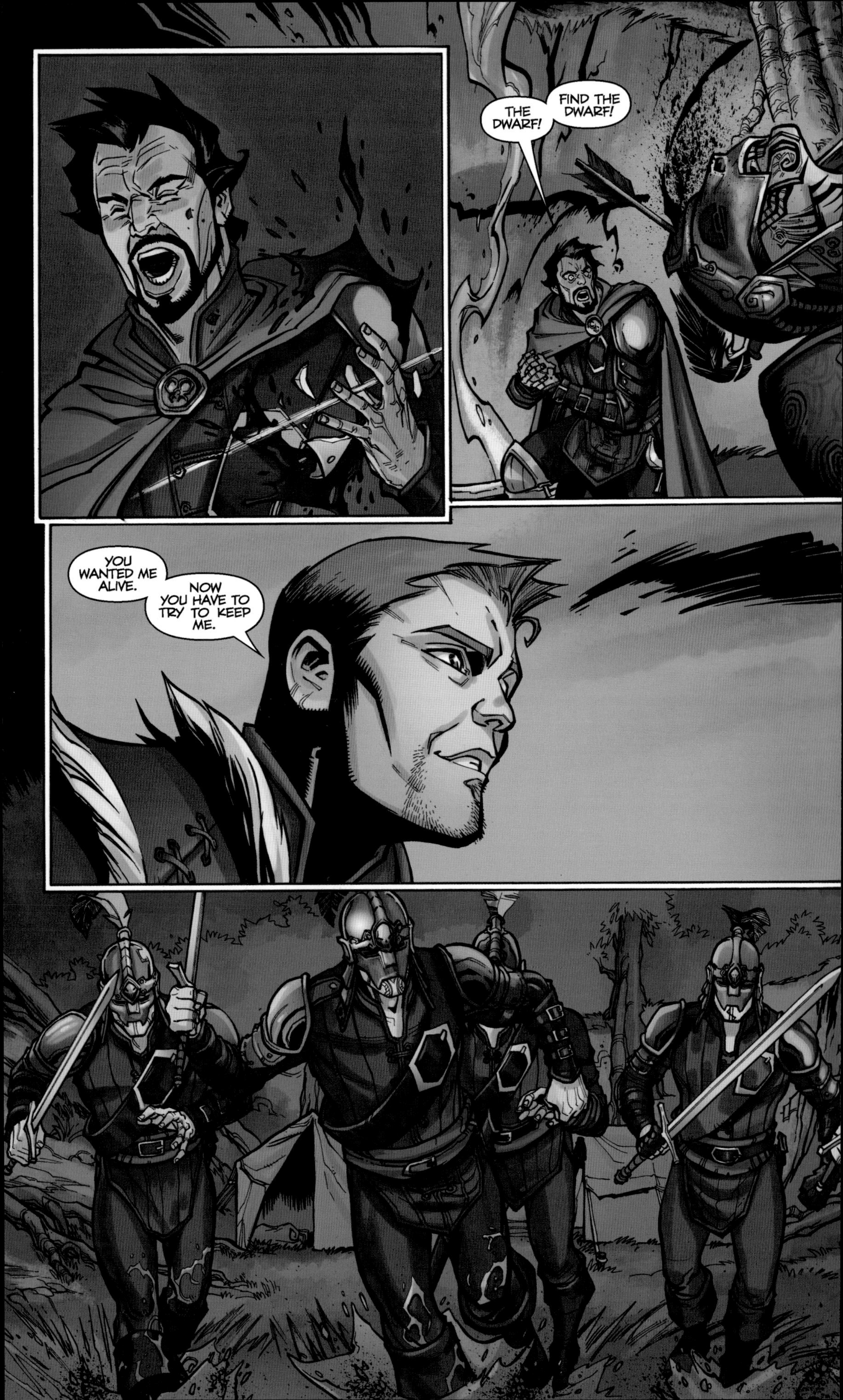
FIND THE DWARF!
THE DWARF!
YOU WANTED ME ALIVE.
NOW YOU HAVE TO TRY TO KEEP ME.

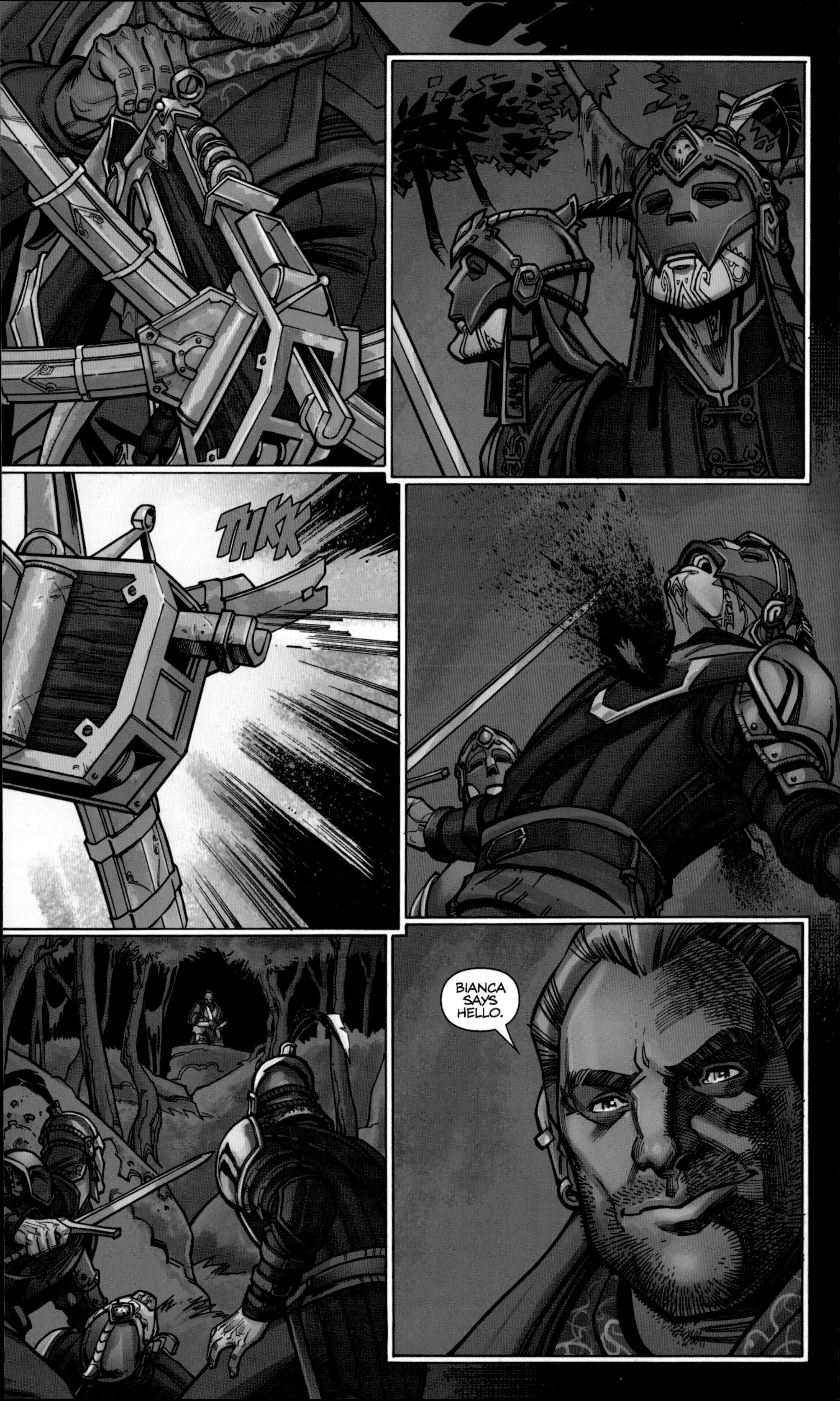
THKK
BIANCA SAYS HELLO.

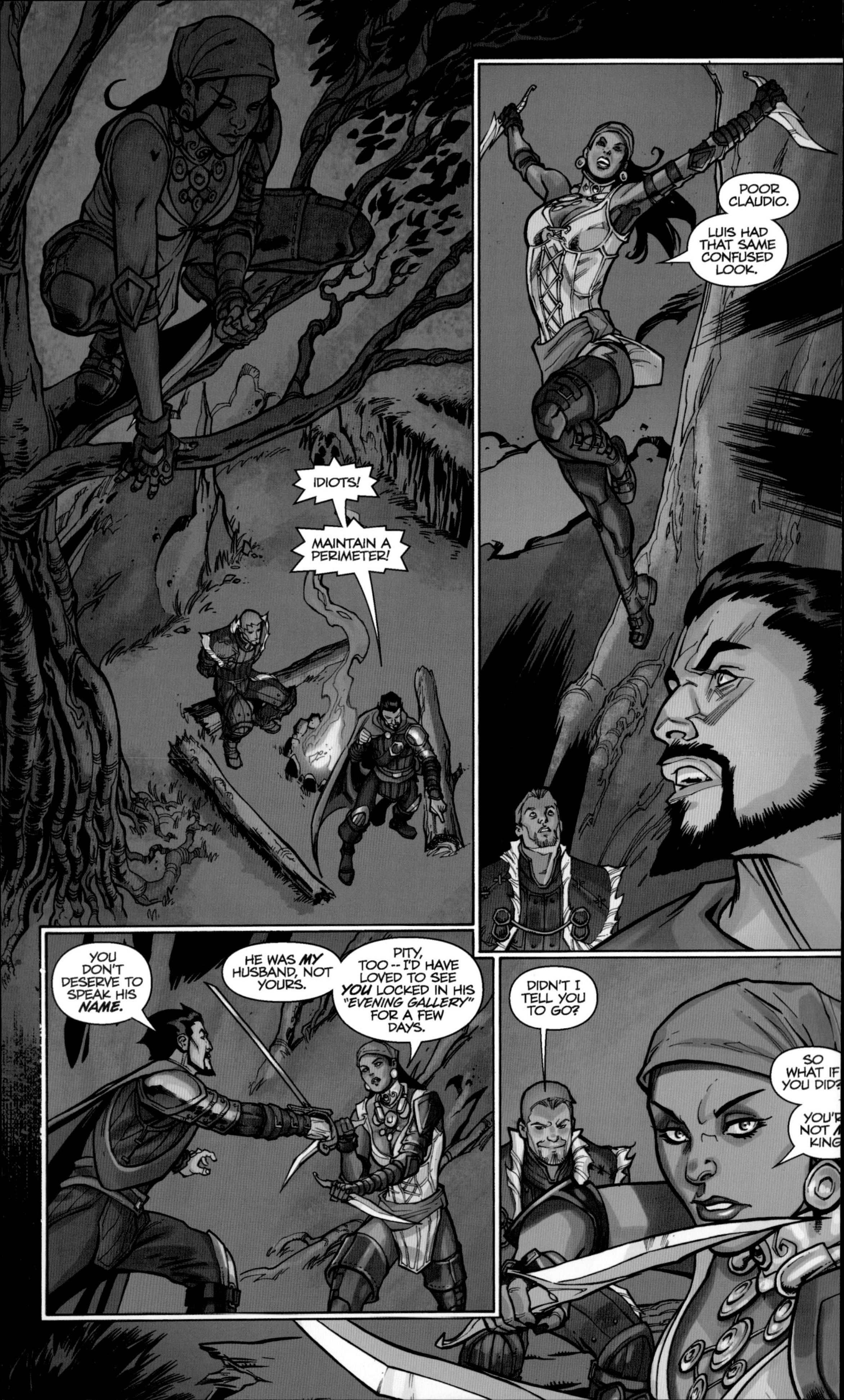
IDIOTS!
MAINTAIN A PERIMETER!
POOR CLAUDIO.
LUIS HAD THAT SAME CONFUSED LOOK.
YOU DON'T DESERVE TO SPEAK HIS NAME.
HE WAS MY HUSBAND, NOT YOURS.
PITY, TOO -- I'D HAVE LOVED TO SEE YOU LOCKED IN HIS "EVENING GALLERY" FOR A FEW DAYS.
DIDN'T I TELL YOU TO GO?
SO WHAT IF YOU DID?
YOU'R NOT KING

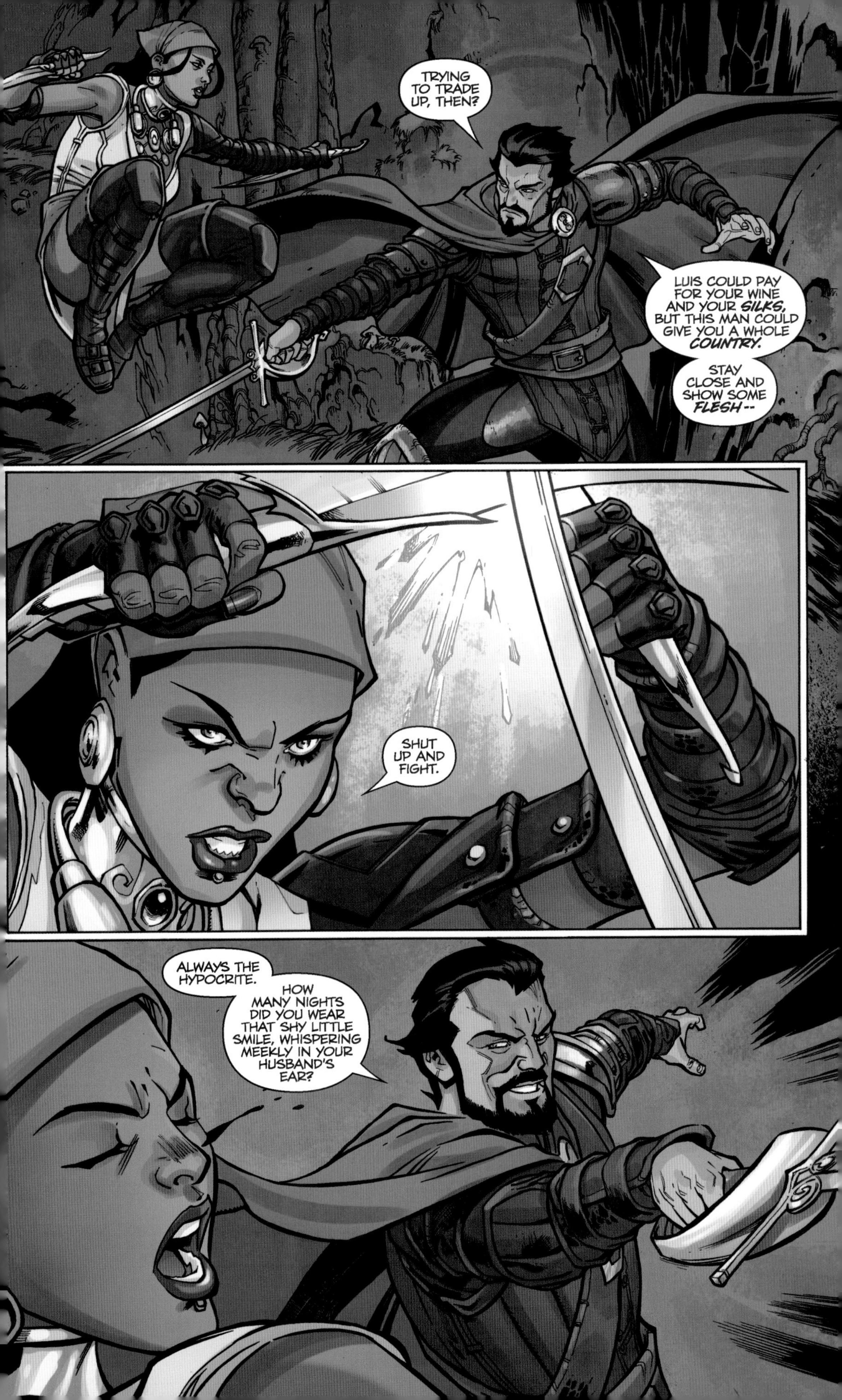
TRYING TO TRADE UP, THEN?
LUIS COULD PAY FOR YOUR WINE AND YOUR SILKS, BUT THIS MAN COULD GIVE YOU A WHOLE COUNTRY.
STAY CLOSE AND SHOW SOME FLESH--
SHUT UP AND FIGHT.
ALWAYS THE HYPOCRITE.
HOW MANY NIGHTS DID YOU WEAR THAT SHY LITTLE SMILE, WHISPERING MEEKLY IN YOUR HUSBAND'S EAR?

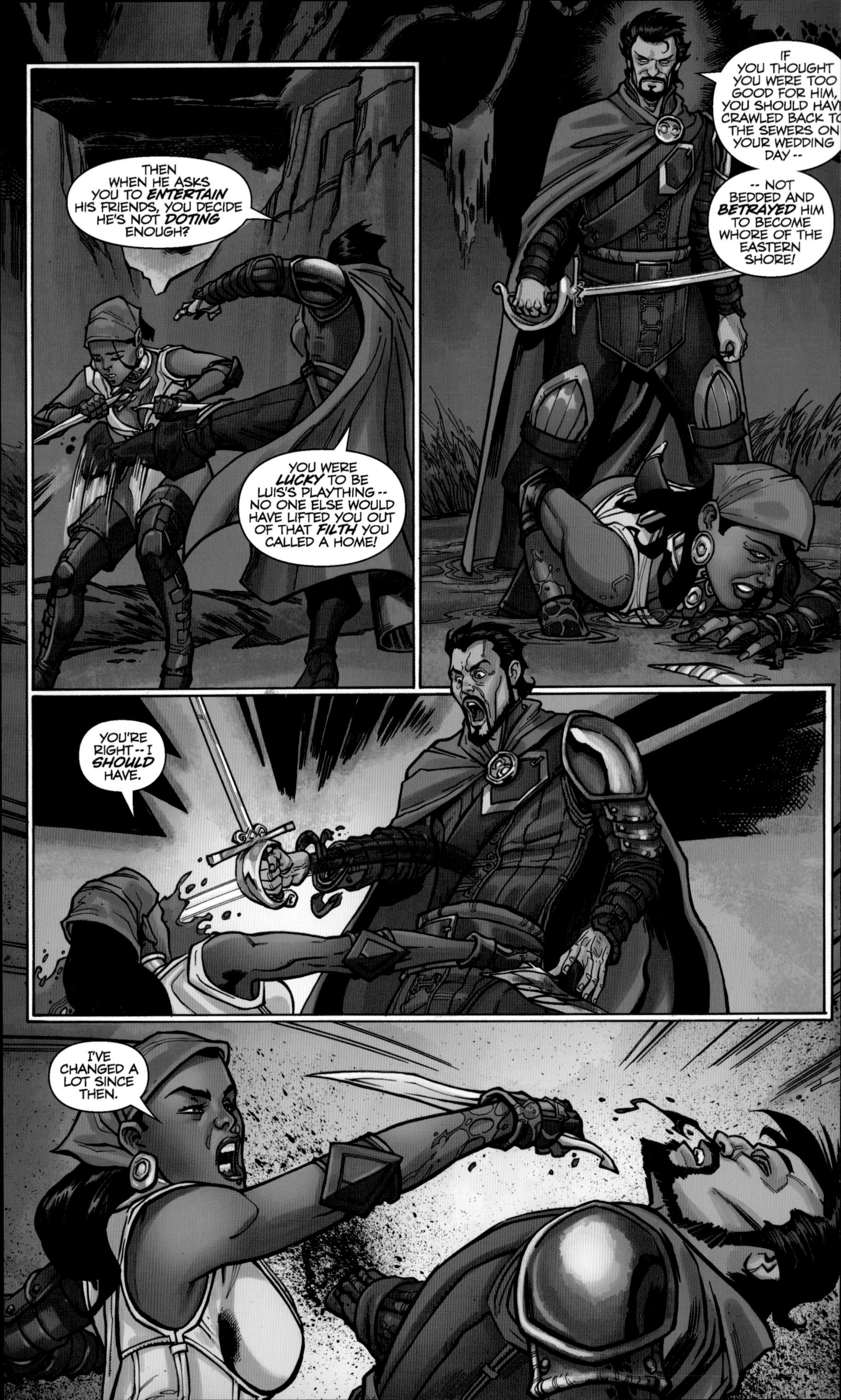
THEN WHEN HE ASKS YOU TO ENTERTAIN HIS FRIENDS, YOU DECIDE HE'S NOT DOTING ENOUGH?
IF YOU THOUGHT YOU WERE TOO GOOD FOR HIM, YOU SHOULD HAVE CRAWLED BACK TO THE SEWERS ON YOUR WEDDING DAY --
-- NOT BEDDED AND BETRAYED HIM TO BECOME WHORE OF THE EASTERN SHORE!
YOU WERE LUCKY TO BE LUIS'S PLAYTHING -- NO ONE ELSE WOULD HAVE LIFTED YOU OUT OF THAT FILTH YOU CALLED A HOME!
YOU'RE RIGHT -- I SHOULD HAVE.
I'VE CHANGED A LOT SINCE THEN.

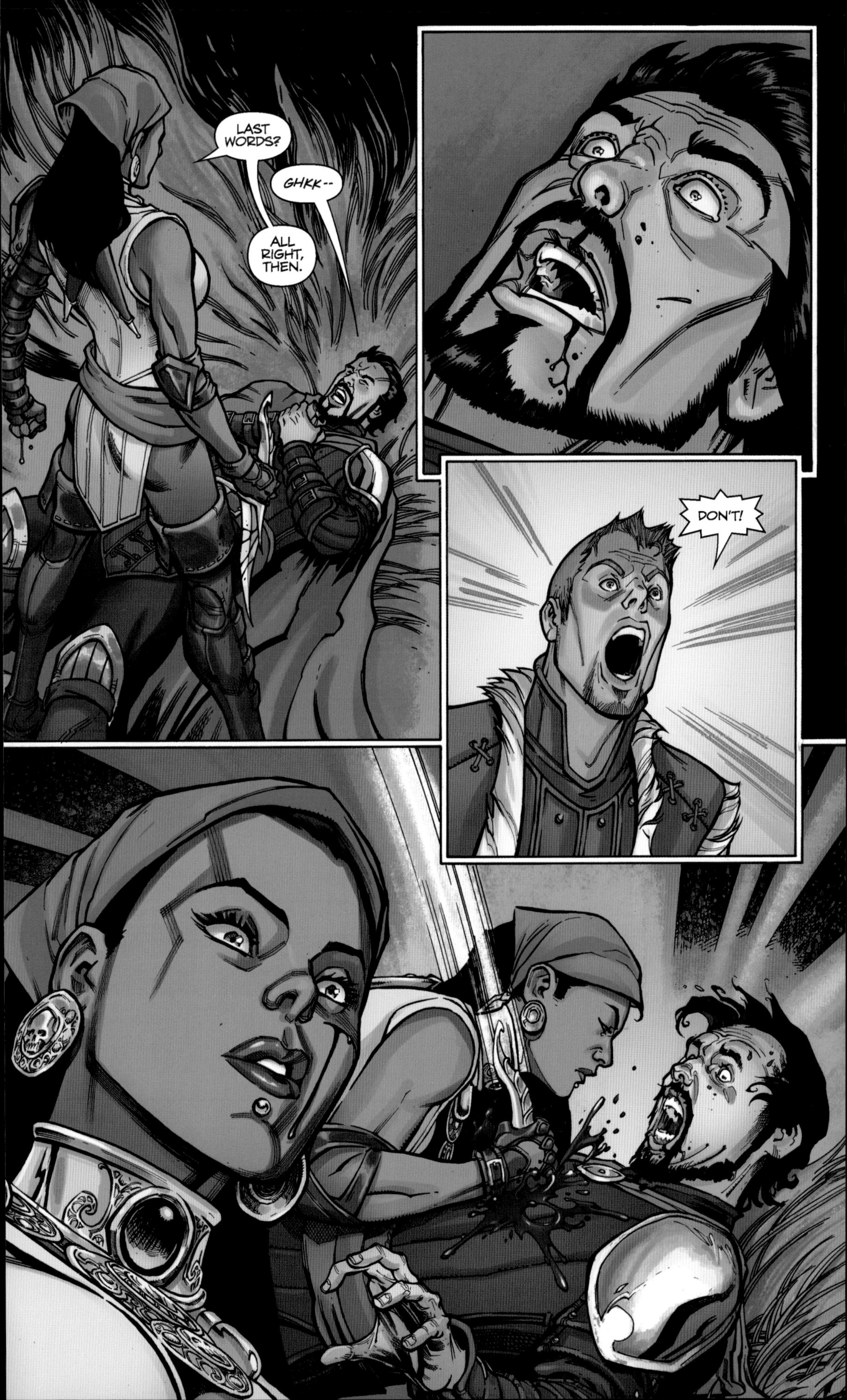
LAST WORDS?
GHKK--
ALL RIGHT, THEN.
DON'T!

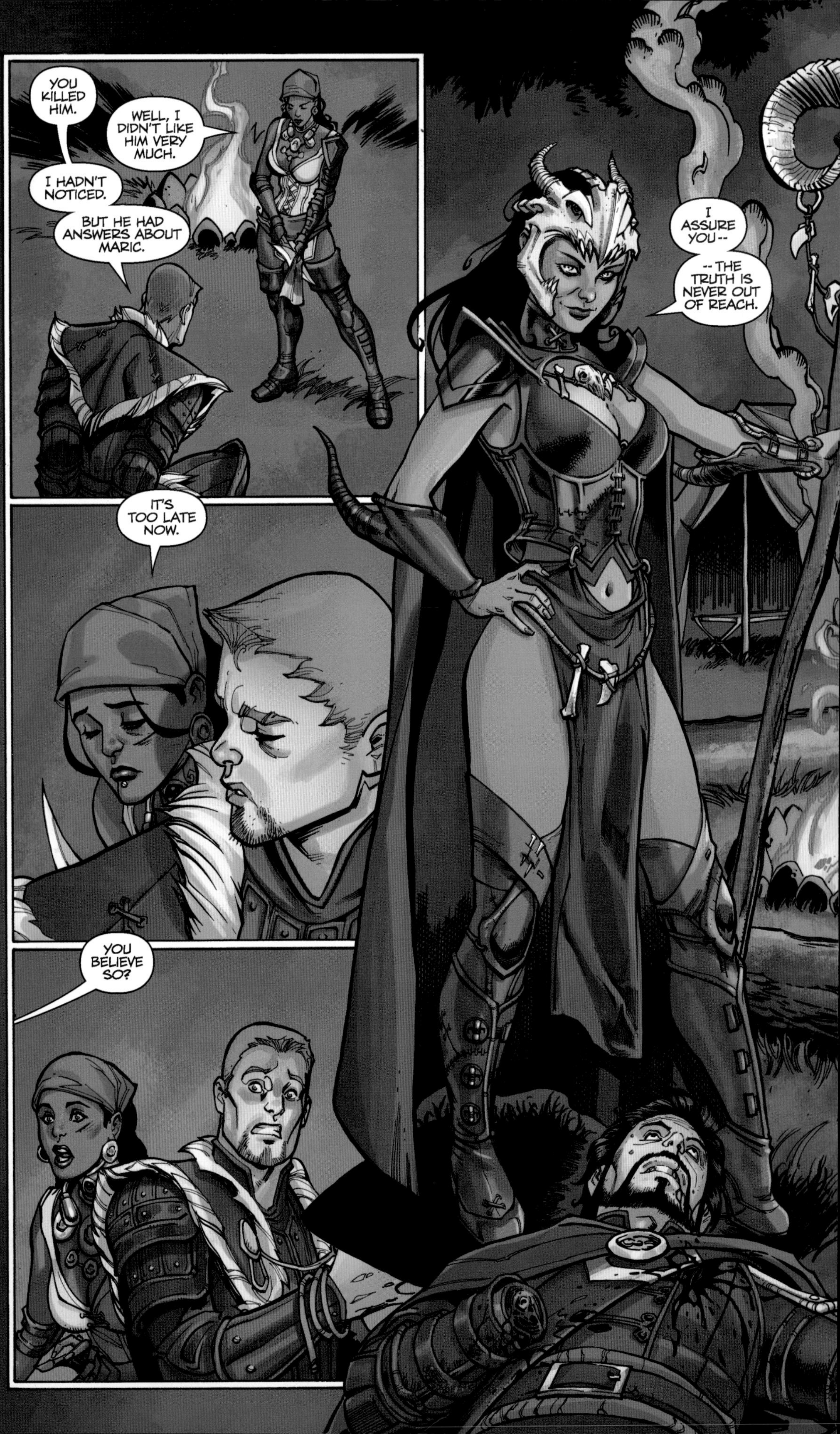
YOU KILLED HIM.
WELL, I DIDN'T LIKE HIM VERY MUCH.
I HADN'T NOTICED.
BUT HE HAD ANSWERS ABOUT MARIC.
I ASSURE YOU--
-- THE TRUTH IS NEVER OUT OF REACH.
IT'S TOO LATE NOW.
YOU BELIEVE SO?

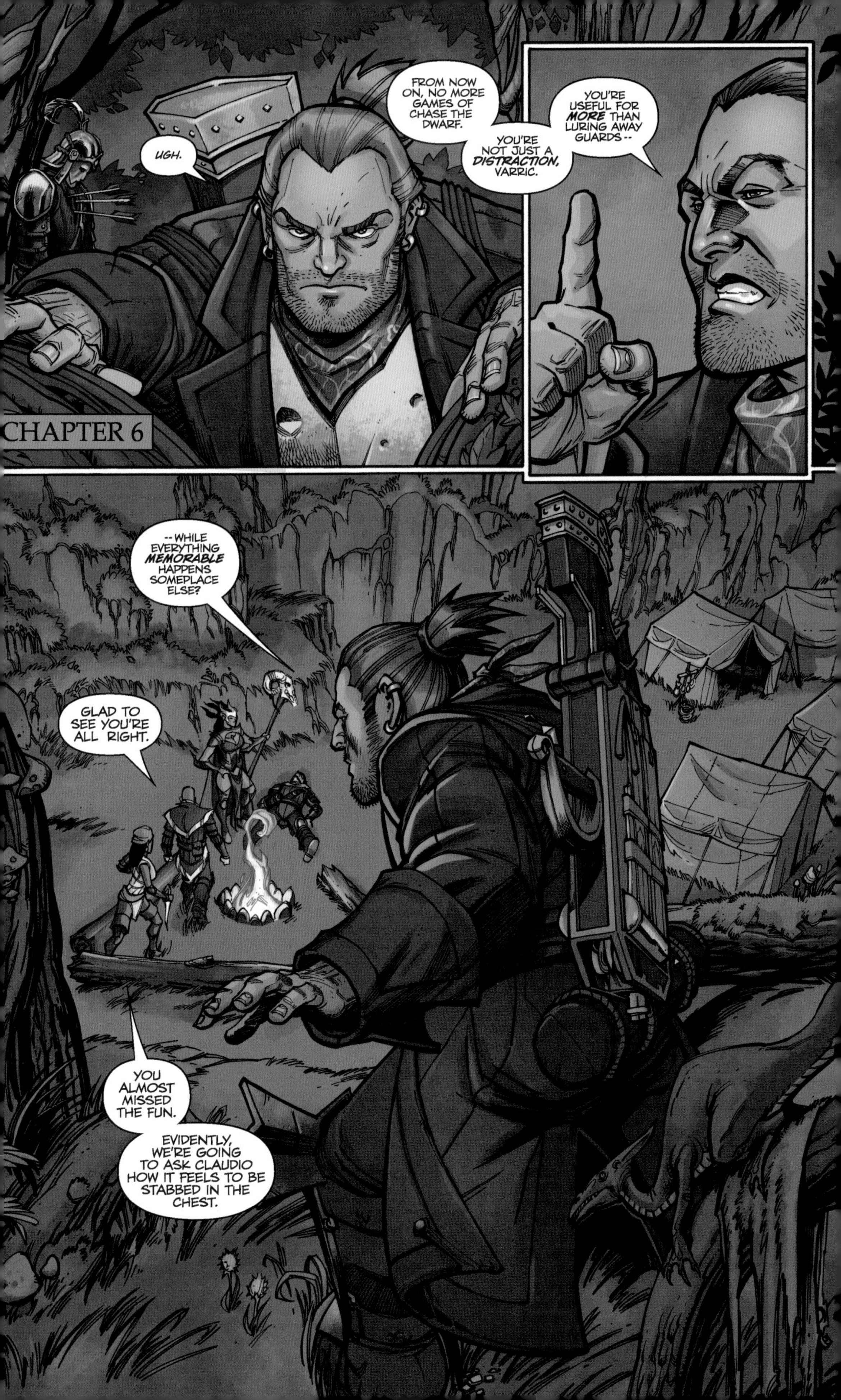
CHAPTER 6
UGH.
FROM NOW ON, NO MORE GAMES OF CHASE THE DWARF.
YOU'RE NOT JUST A DISTRACTION, VARRIC.
YOU'RE USEFUL FOR MORE THAN LURING AWAY GUARDS --
-- WHILE EVERYTHING MEMORABLE HAPPENS SOMEPLACE ELSE?
GLAD TO SEE YOU'RE ALL RIGHT.
YOU ALMOST MISSED THE FUN.
EVIDENTLY, WE'RE GOING TO ASK CLAUDIO HOW IT FEELS TO BE STABBED IN THE CHEST.

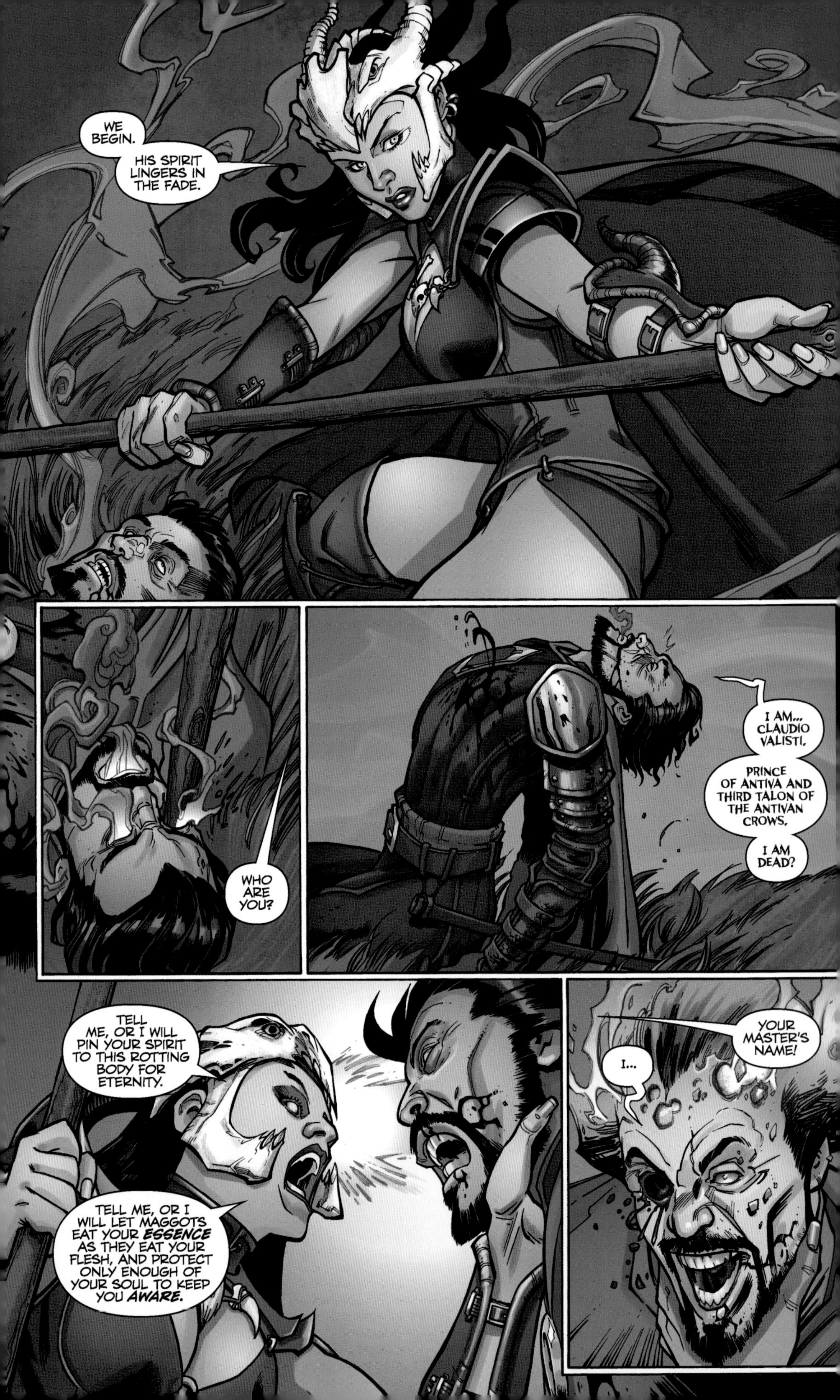
WE BEGIN.
HIS SPIRIT LINGERS IN THE FADE.
WHO ARE YOU?
I AM... CLAUDIO VALISTI,
PRINCE OF ANTIVA AND THIRD TALON OF THE ANTIVAN CROWS.
I AM DEAD?
TELL ME, OR I WILL PIN YOUR SPIRIT TO THIS ROTTING BODY FOR ETERNITY.
TELL ME, OR I WILL LET MAGGOTS EAT YOUR ESSENCE AS THEY EAT YOUR FLESH, AND PROTECT ONLY ENOUGH OF YOUR SOUL TO KEEP YOU AWARE.
YOUR MASTER'S NAME!
I...

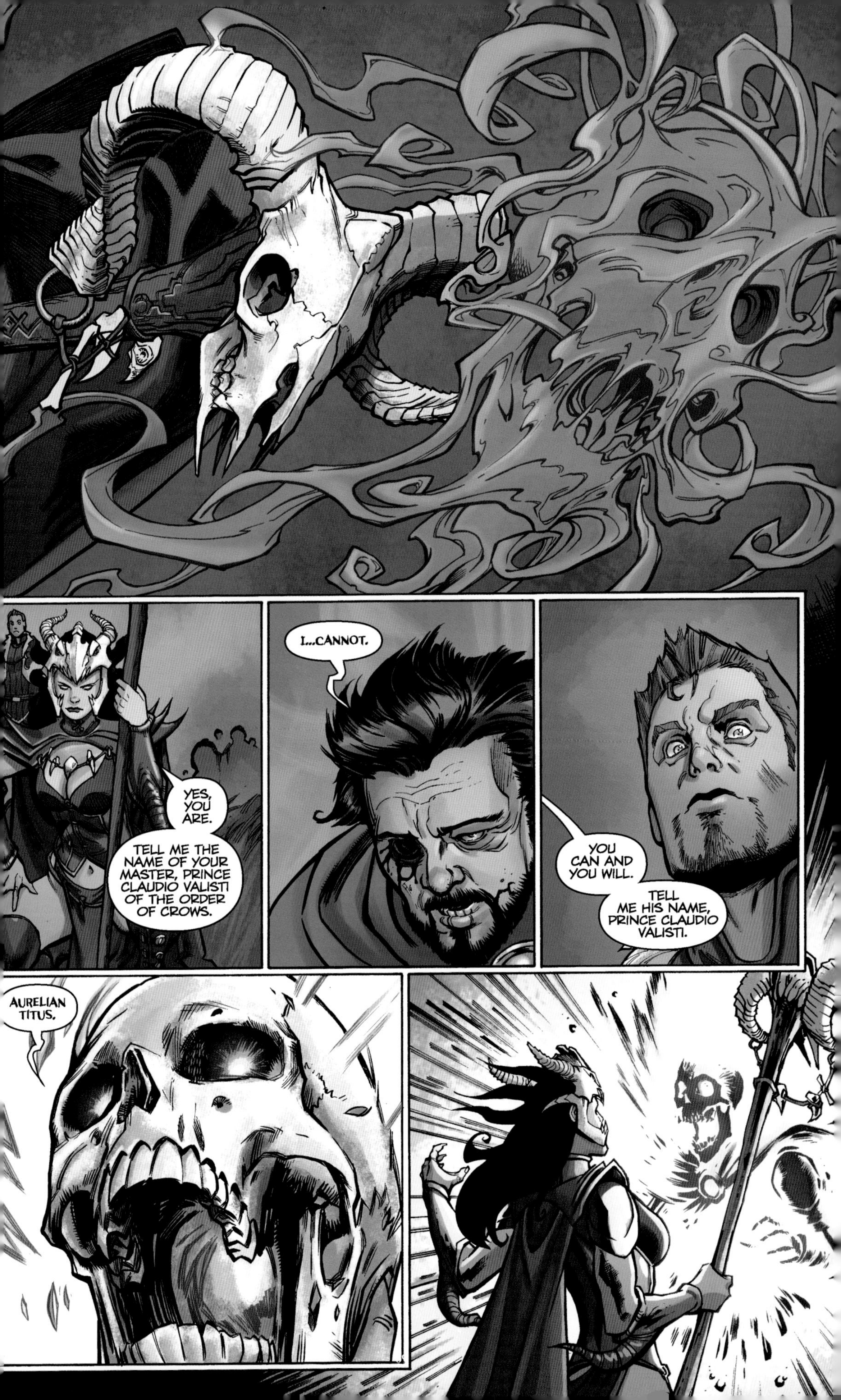

YES, YOU ARE.
TELL ME THE NAME OF YOUR MASTER, PRINCE CLAUDIO VALISTI OF THE ORDER OF CROWS.
I...CANNOT.
YOU CAN AND YOU WILL.
TELL ME HIS NAME, PRINCE CLAUDIO VALISTI.
AURELIAN TITUS.

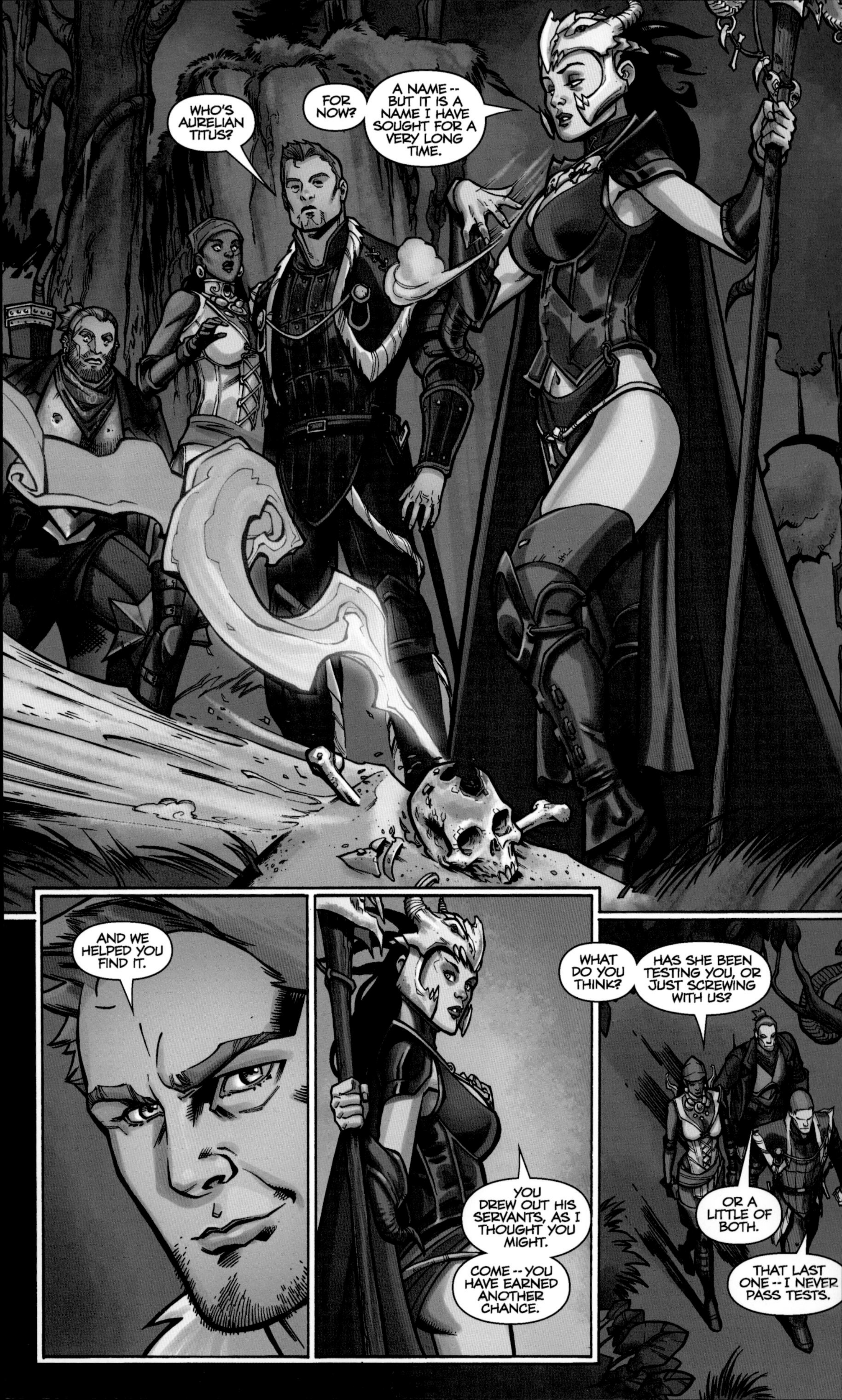
WHO'S AURELIAN TITUS?
FOR NOW?
A NAME -- BUT IT IS A NAME I HAVE SOUGHT FOR A VERY LONG TIME.
AND WE HELPED YOU FIND IT.
YOU DREW OUT HIS SERVANTS, AS I THOUGHT YOU MIGHT.
COME -- YOU HAVE EARNED ANOTHER CHANCE.
WHAT DO YOU THINK?
HAS SHE BEEN TESTING YOU, OR JUST SCREWING WITH US?
OR A LITTLE OF BOTH.
THAT LAST ONE -- I NEVER PASS TESTS.

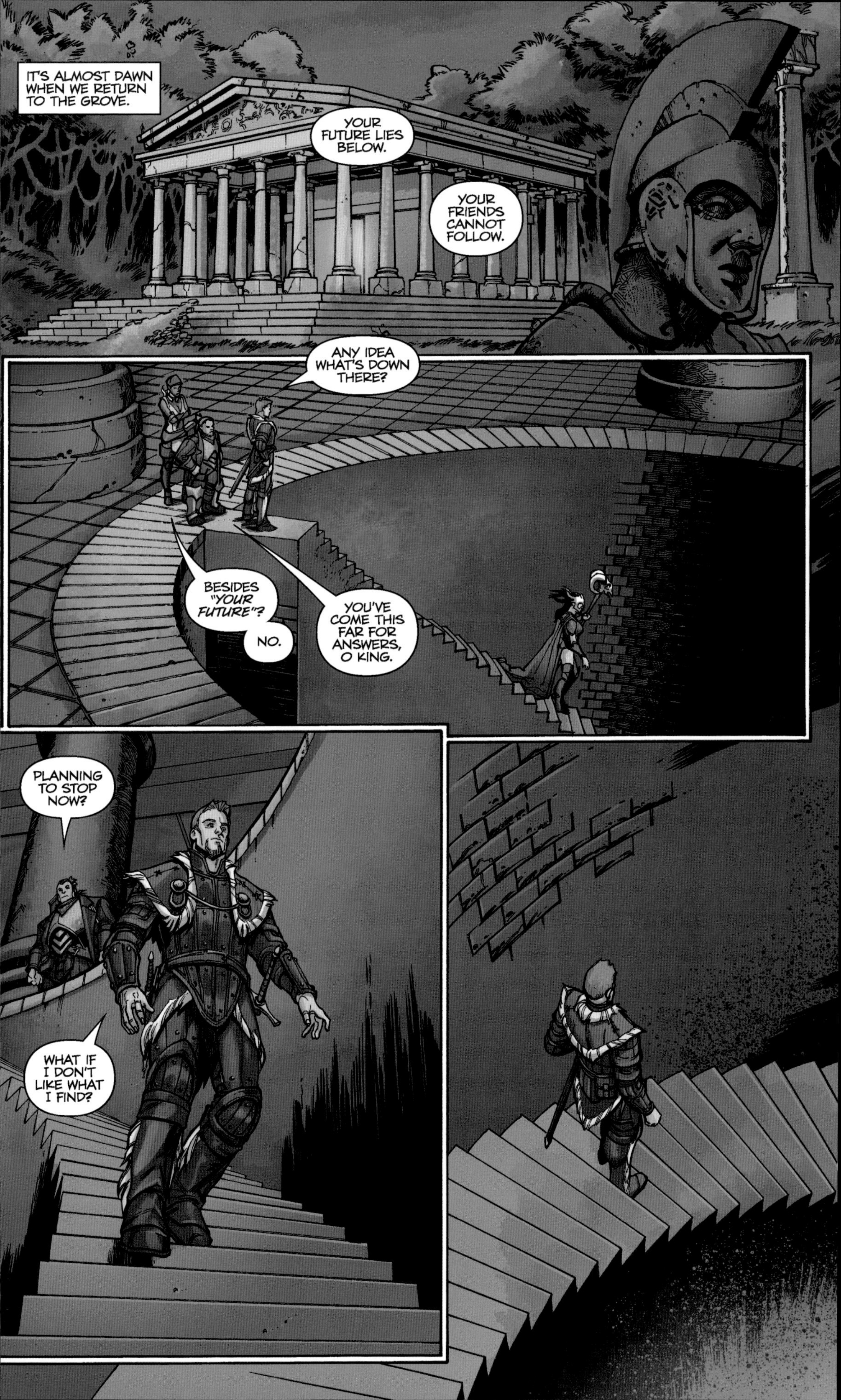
IT'S ALMOST DAWN WHEN WE RETURN TO THE GROVE.
YOUR FUTURE LIES BELOW.
YOUR FRIENDS CANNOT FOLLOW.
ANY IDEA WHAT'S DOWN THERE?
BESIDES "YOUR FUTURE"?
NO.
YOU'VE COME THIS FAR FOR ANSWERS, O KING.
PLANNING TO STOP NOW?
WHAT IF I DON'T LIKE WHAT I FIND?

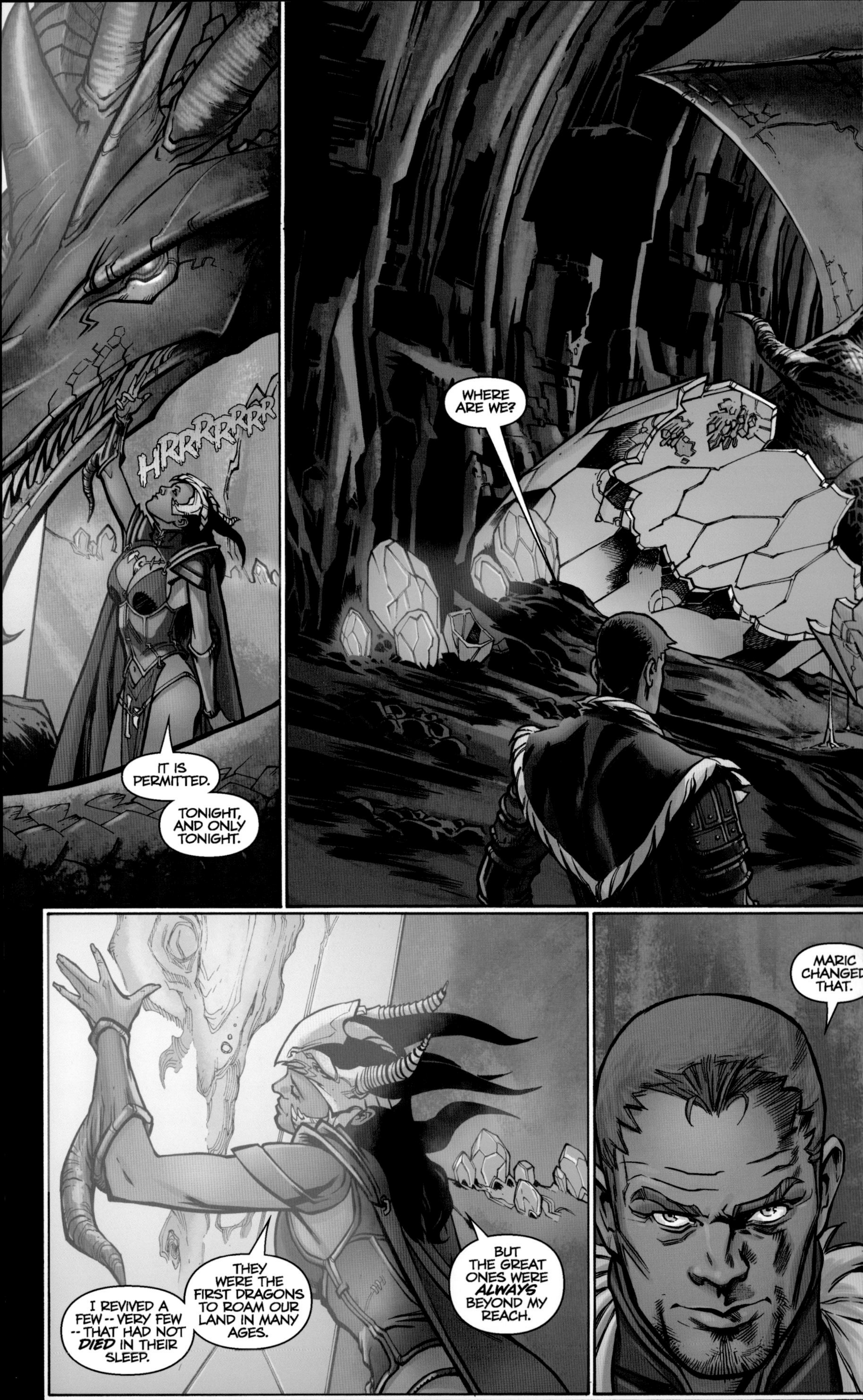
HRRRRRRR
IT IS PERMITTED.
TONIGHT, AND ONLY TONIGHT.
WHERE ARE WE?
I REVIVED A FEW -- VERY FEW -- THAT HAD NOT DIED IN THEIR SLEEP.
THEY WERE THE FIRST DRAGONS TO ROAM OUR LAND IN MANY AGES.
BUT THE GREAT ONES WERE ALWAYS BEYOND MY REACH.
MARIC CHANGED THAT.

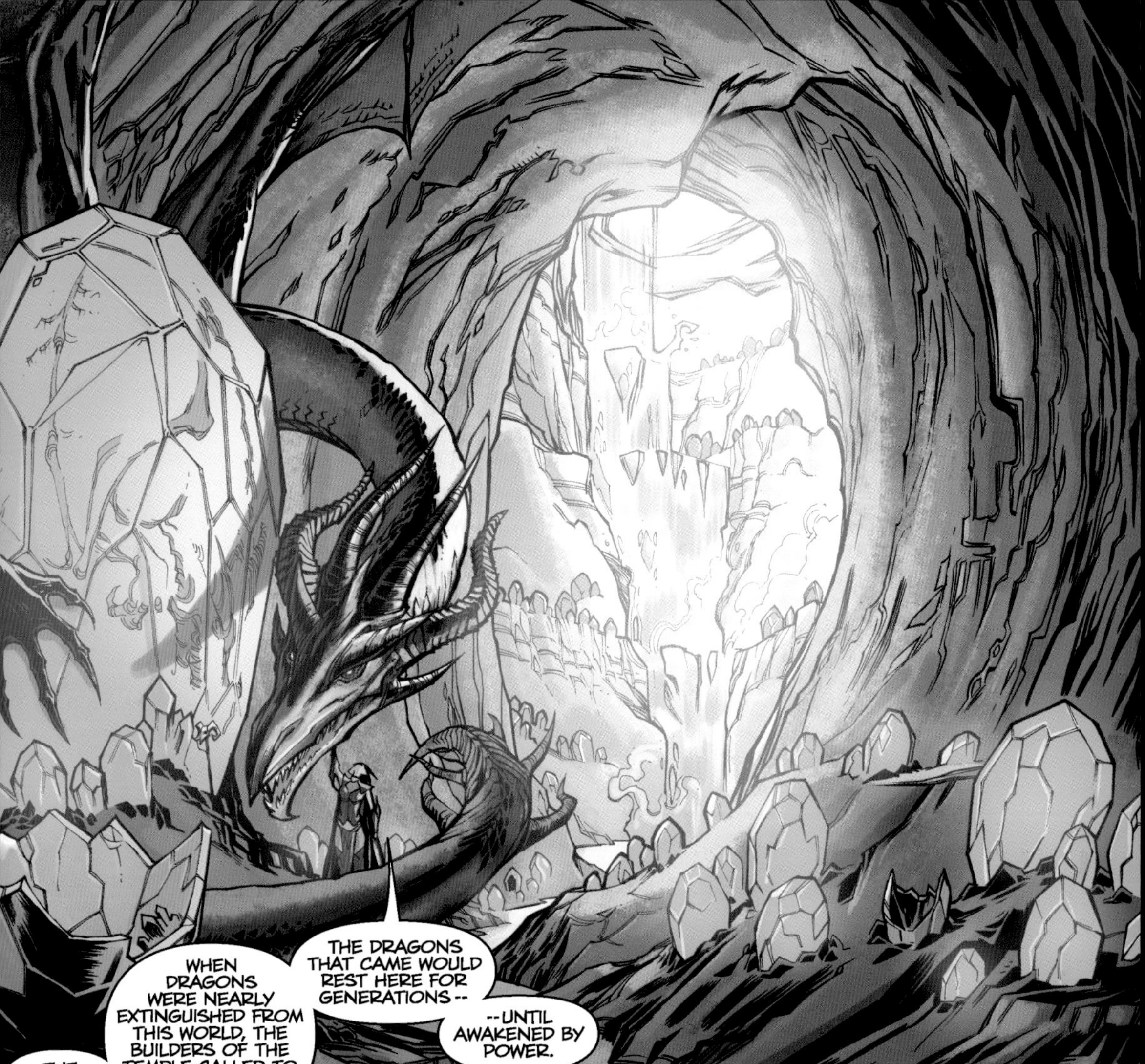
THE HALL OF SLEEPERS.
WHEN DRAGONS WERE NEARLY EXTINGUISHED FROM THIS WORLD, THE BUILDERS OF THE TEMPLE CALLED TO THE FEW THAT REMAINED.
THE DRAGONS THAT CAME WOULD REST HERE FOR GENERATIONS --
--UNTIL AWAKENED BY POWER.

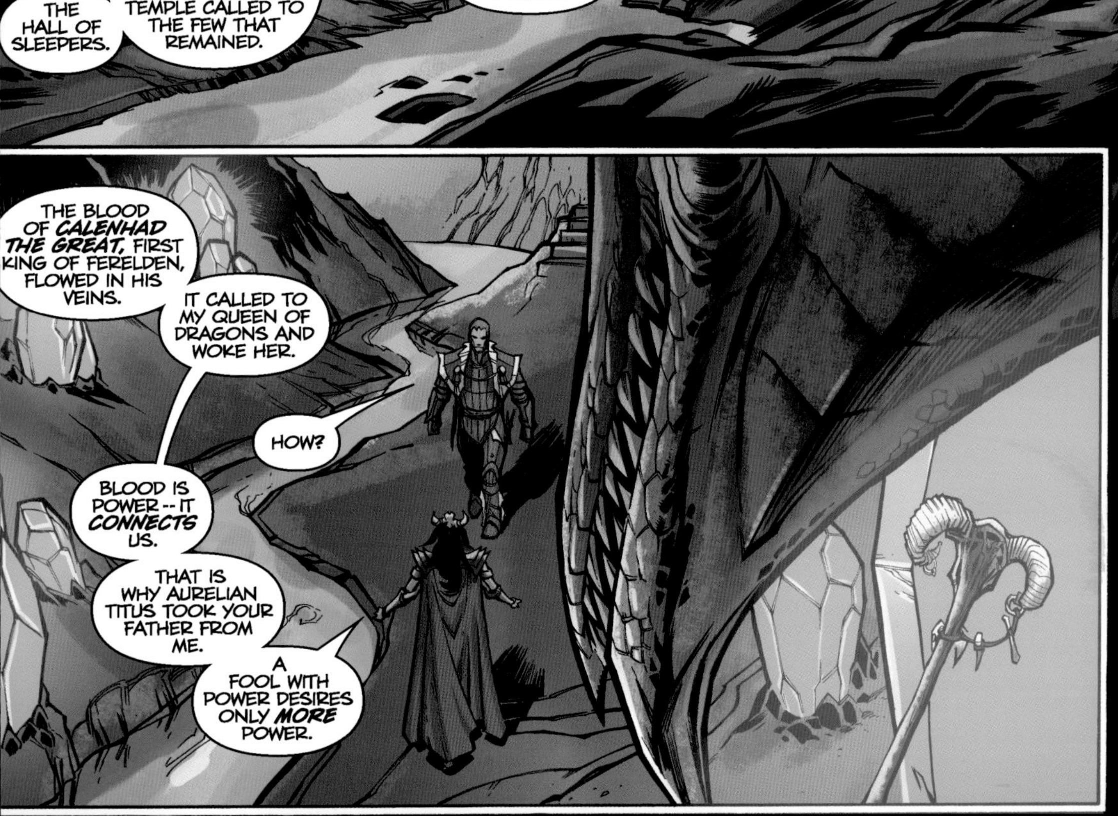
THE BLOOD OF *CALENHAD THE GREAT,* FIRST KING OF FERELDEN, FLOWED IN HIS VEINS.
IT CALLED TO MY QUEEN OF DRAGONS AND WOKE HER.
HOW?
BLOOD IS POWER -- IT *CONNECTS* US.
THAT IS WHY AURELIAN TITUS TOOK YOUR FATHER FROM ME.
A FOOL WITH POWER DESIRES ONLY *MORE* POWER.

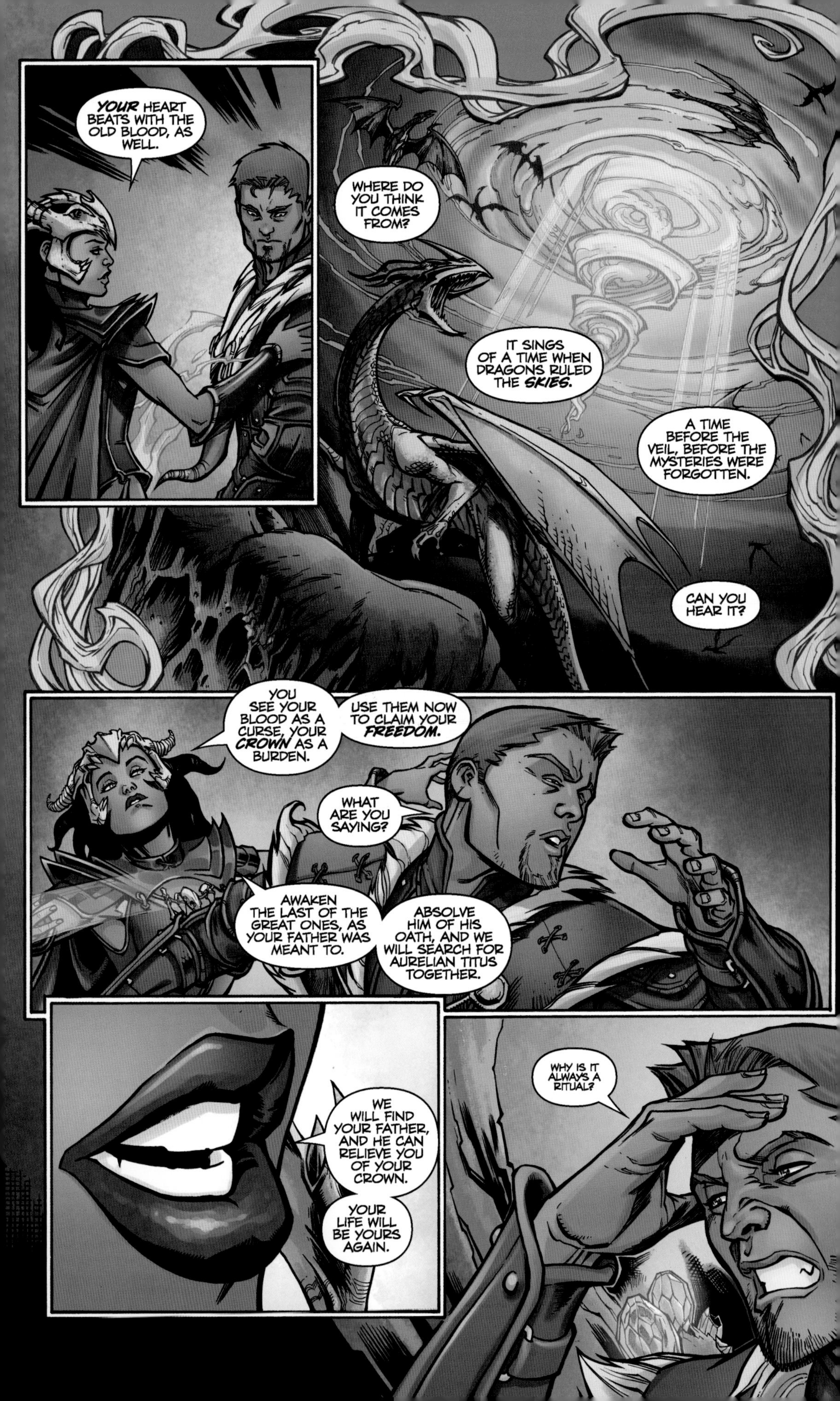
YOUR HEART BEATS WITH THE OLD BLOOD, AS WELL.
WHERE DO YOU THINK IT COMES FROM?
IT SINGS OF A TIME WHEN DRAGONS RULED THE SKIES.
A TIME BEFORE THE VEIL, BEFORE THE MYSTERIES WERE FORGOTTEN.
CAN YOU HEAR IT?
YOU SEE YOUR BLOOD AS A CURSE, YOUR CROWN AS A BURDEN.
USE THEM NOW TO CLAIM YOUR FREEDOM.
WHAT ARE YOU SAYING?
AWAKEN THE LAST OF THE GREAT ONES, AS YOUR FATHER WAS MEANT TO.
ABSOLVE HIM OF HIS OATH, AND WE WILL SEARCH FOR AURELIAN TITUS TOGETHER.
WE WILL FIND YOUR FATHER, AND HE CAN RELIEVE YOU OF YOUR CROWN.
YOUR LIFE WILL BE YOURS AGAIN.
WHY IS IT ALWAYS A RITUAL?

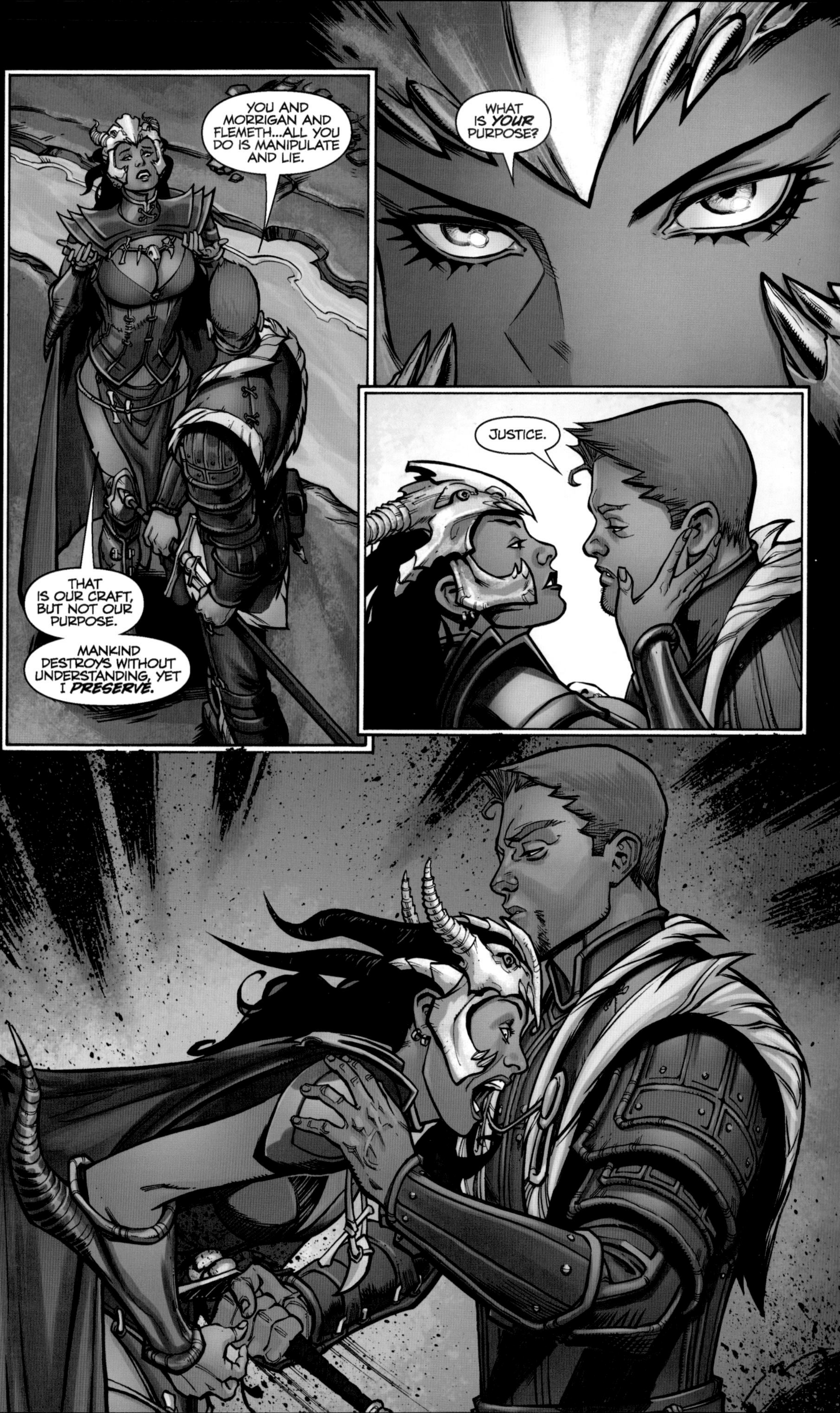
YOU AND MORRIGAN AND FLEMETH...ALL YOU DO IS MANIPULATE AND LIE.
THAT IS OUR CRAFT, BUT NOT OUR PURPOSE.
MANKIND DESTROYS WITHOUT UNDERSTANDING, YET I PRESERVE.
WHAT IS YOUR PURPOSE?
JUSTICE.

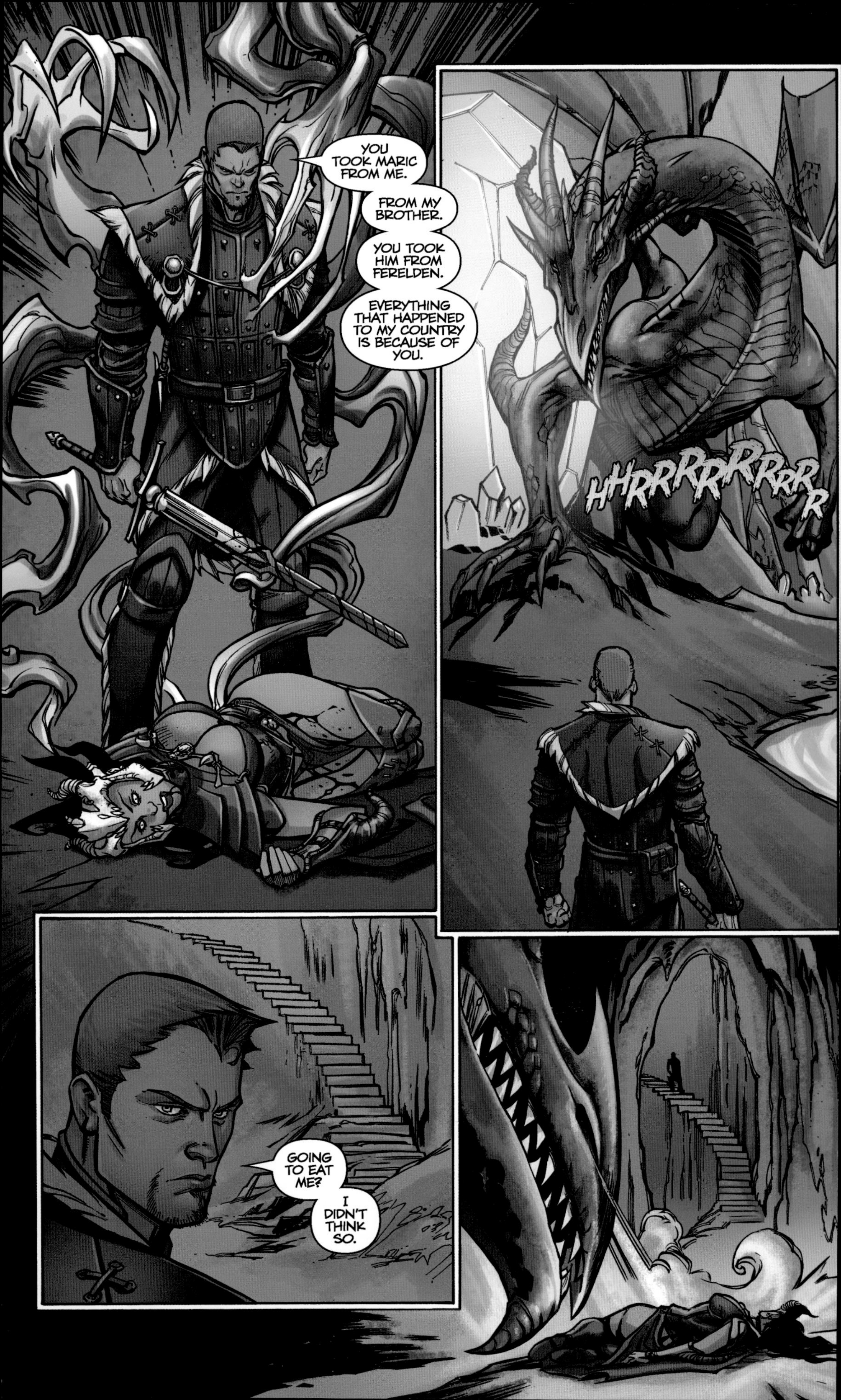
YOU TOOK MARIC FROM ME.
FROM MY BROTHER.
YOU TOOK HIM FROM FERELDEN.
EVERYTHING THAT HAPPENED TO MY COUNTRY IS BECAUSE OF YOU.
HHRRRRRRRRRR
GOING TO EAT ME?
I DIDN'T THINK SO.

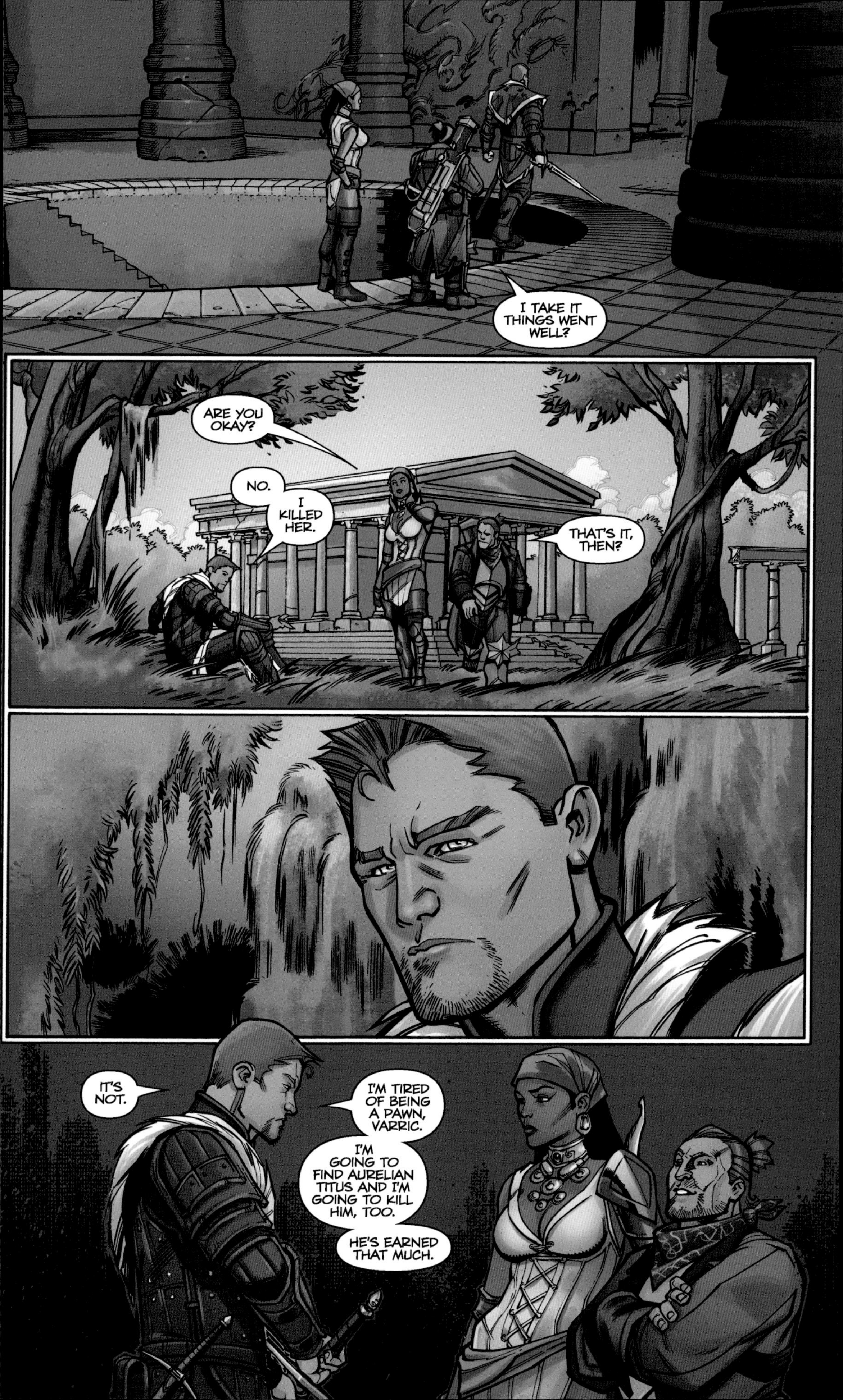
I TAKE IT THINGS WENT WELL?
ARE YOU OKAY?
NO.
I KILLED HER.
THAT'S IT, THEN?
IT'S NOT.
I'M TIRED OF BEING A PAWN, VARRIC.
I'M GOING TO FIND AURELIAN TITUS AND I'M GOING TO KILL HIM, TOO.
HE'S EARNED THAT MUCH.

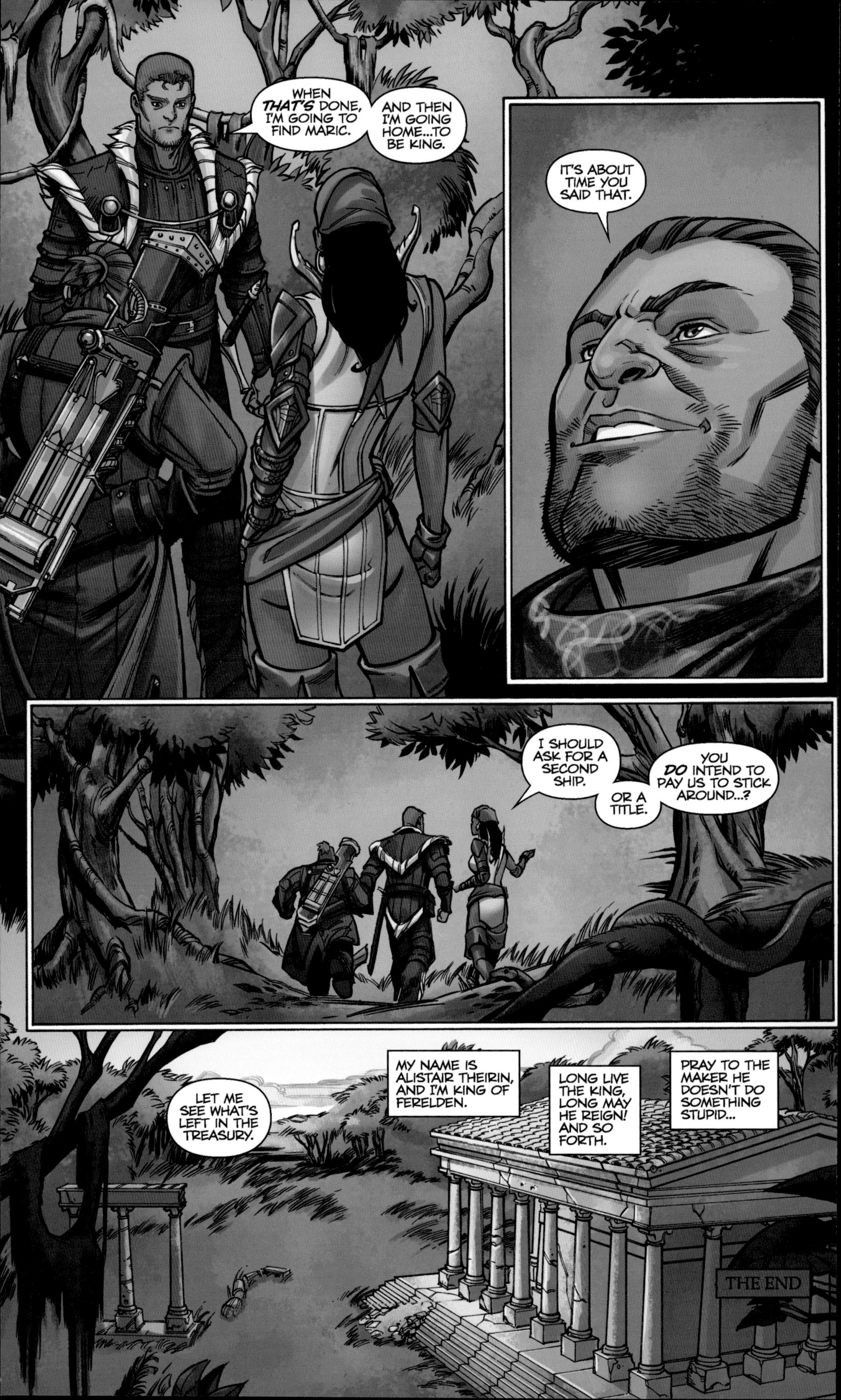
WHEN THAT'S DONE, I'M GOING TO FIND MARIC.
AND THEN I'M GOING HOME...TO BE KING.
IT'S ABOUT TIME YOU SAID THAT.
I SHOULD ASK FOR A SECOND SHIP.
OR A TITLE.
YOU DO INTEND TO PAY US TO STICK AROUND...?
LET ME SEE WHAT'S LEFT IN THE TREASURY.
MY NAME IS ALISTAIR THEIRIN, AND I'M KING OF FERELDEN.
LONG LIVE THE KING, LONG MAY HE REIGN! AND SO FORTH.
PRAY TO THE MAKER HE DOESN'T DO SOMETHING STUPID...
THE END

EXPLORE THE MASS EFFECT UNIVERSE WITH DARK HORSE!

Created in close collaboration with BioWare and the writers and artists of the games, Dark Horse's *Mass Effect* graphic novels and merchandise are essential companions to gaming's deepest universe!

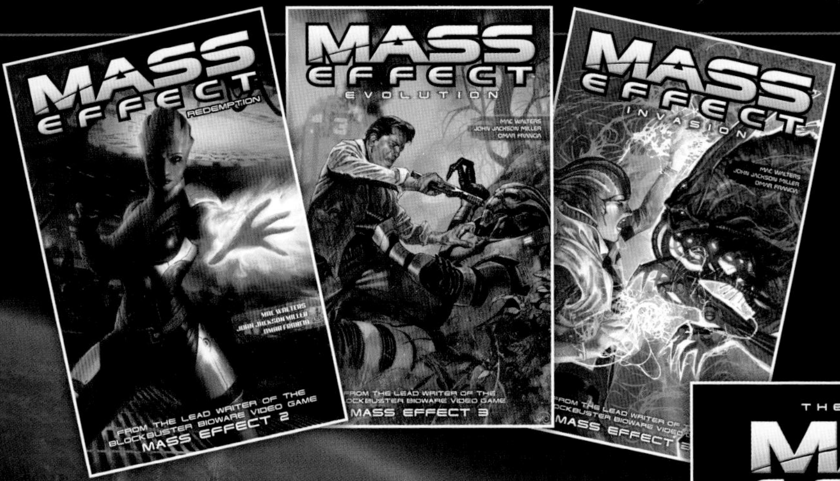
MASS EFFECT
REDEMPTION
MAC WALTERS
JOHN JACKSON MILLER
OMAR FRANCIA
FROM THE LEAD WRITER OF THE BLOCKBUSTER BIOWARE VIDEO GAME
MASS EFFECT 2
MASS EFFECT
EVOLUTION
MAC WALTERS
JOHN JACKSON MILLER
OMAR FRANCIA
FROM THE LEAD WRITER OF THE BLOCKBUSTER BIOWARE VIDEO GAME
MASS EFFECT 3
MASS EFFECT
INVASION
MAC WALTERS
JOHN JACKSON MILLER
OMAR FRANCIA

MASS EFFECT: REDEMPTION
ISBN 978-59582-481-3

MASS EFFECT: EVOLUTION
ISBN 978-59582-759-3

MASS EFFECT: INVASION
ISBN 978-59582-867-5

$16.99 EACH

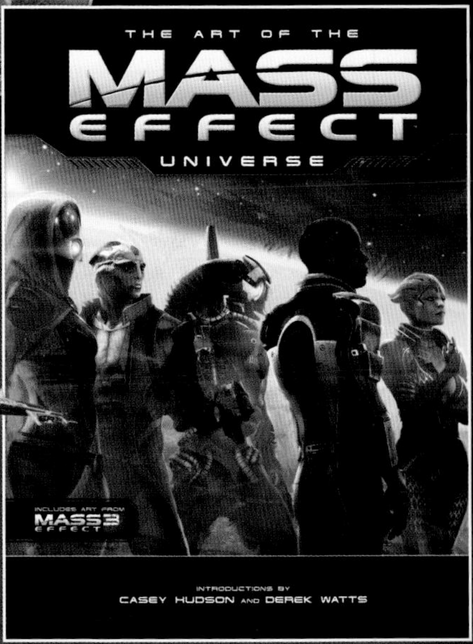
THE ART OF THE
MASS EFFECT
UNIVERSE
INCLUDES ART FROM
MASS 3 EFFECT
INTRODUCTIONS BY
CASEY HUDSON AND DEREK WATTS

ART OF THE MASS EFFECT UNIVERSE
ISBN 978-59582-768-5 | **$39.99**

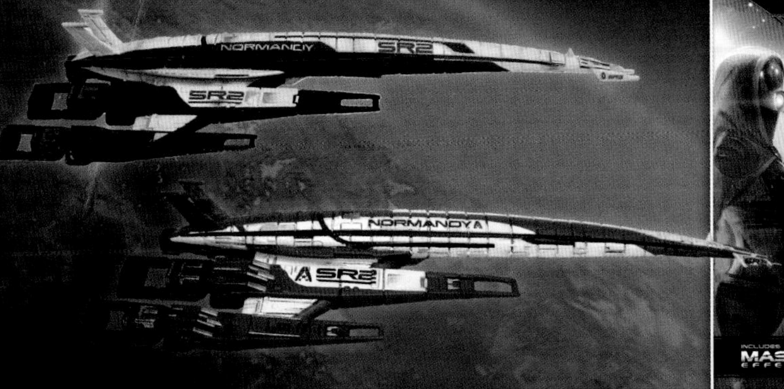
NORMANDY
SR2
NORMANDY
SR2

CERBERUS NORMANDY SR-2 SHIP REPLICA
ISBN 978-61659-207-3

ALLIANCE NORMANDY SR-2 SHIP REPLICA
ISBN 978-61659-161-8

$34.99 EACH

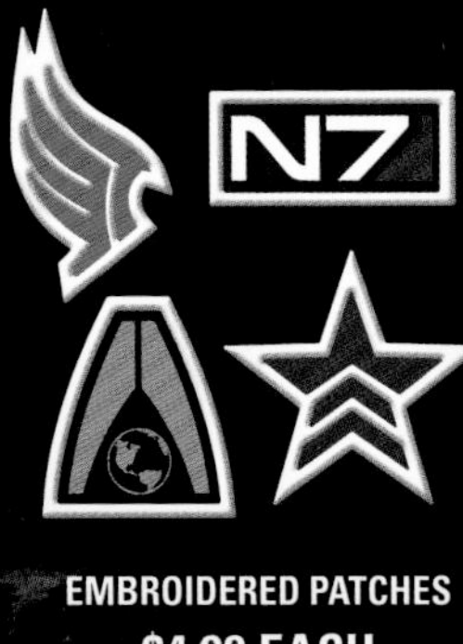
N7

EMBROIDERED PATCHES
$4.99 EACH

PARAGON
ISBN 978-1-61659-246-2

N7 LOGO
ISBN 978-1-61659-245-5

SYSTEM ALLIANCE
ISBN 978-1-61659-248-6

RENEGADE
ISBN 978-1-61659-247-9

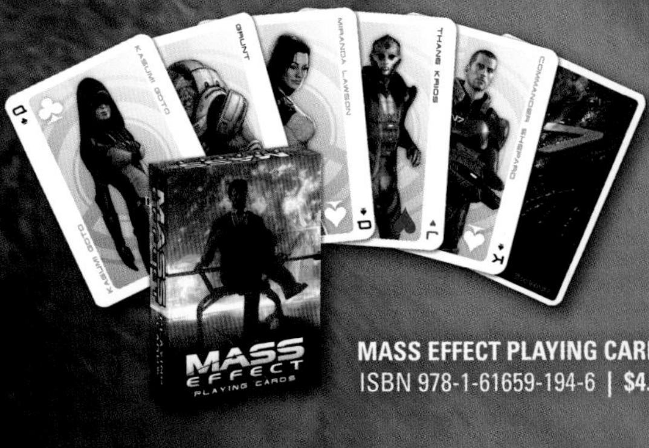
KASUMI GOTO
GRUNT
MIRANDA LAWSON
THANE KRIOS
COMMANDER SHEPARD
MASS EFFECT
PLAYING CARDS

MASS EFFECT PLAYING CARDS
ISBN 978-1-61659-194-6 | **$4.99**

DARK HORSE BOOKS

DarkHorse.com
MassEffect.com

AVAILABLE AT YOUR LOCAL COMICS SHOP OR BOOKSTORE!
To find a comics shop in your area, call 1-888-266-4226
For more information or to order direct: • On the web: DarkHorse.com
• E-mail: mailorder@darkhorse.com • Phone: 1-800-862-0052 Mon.–Fri. 9 AM to 5 PM Pacific Time